Published by
Periplus Editions (HK) Ltd.
with editorial offices at
153 Milk Street
Boston, MA 02109
and
5 Little Road #08-01
Singapore 536983

ISBN: 962-593-268-2

LCC Number: 99-050252

Publisher: Eric Oey
Editors: Jeanine Caunt and Philip Tatham
Production: Violet Wong

Photo Credits:
All photography by Nelli Sheffer. Additional
photos courtesy Miskal-Yedioth Acharonoth
Books (pages 14, 15, 17, 19), Holyland Photo
Libary: Hanan Isachar (page 2) and Modan
Publishing House Ltd (page 4).

Acknowledgments:
The publisher gratefully acknowledges the
assistance of Irit Lilian.

Distributors

North America, Latin America, Europe and the Middle East
Tuttle Publishing
Distrbution Center
Airport Industrial Park
364 Innovation Drive
North Clarendon, VT 05759-9436
Tel: (802) 773-8930
Tel: (800) 526-2778

Japan
Tuttle Publishing
RK Building, 2nd Floor
2-13-10 Shimo-Meguro, Meguro-Ku
Tokyo 153 0064
Tel: (03) 5437-0171
Fax: (03) 5437-0755

Asia-Pacific
Berkeley Books Pte. Ltd.
5 Little Road #08-01
Singapore 536983
Tel: (65) 280-1330
Fax: (65) 280-6290

First Edition
1 3 5 7 9 10 8 6 4 2
07 06 05 04 03 02 01 00
PRINTED IN SINGAPORE

THE FOOD OF
ISRAEL

Authentic Recipes from the Land of Milk and Honey

Text and recipes by Sherry Ansky
Photography by Nelli Sheffer
Editing by Beth Elon
Styling by Nurit Branizky

PERIPLUS

Contents

PART ONE: FOOD IN ISRAEL

Introduction 5
Three Thousand Years of Culinary History 6
The Land of Milk and Honey 11
Religion and Food in the Holy Land 15
Markets & Street Food 21
The New Israeli Cuisine 24

PART TWO: COOKING IN ISRAEL

The Israeli Kitchen 29
Israeli Ingredients 31

PART THREE: THE RECIPES

Basic Recipes 35
Salads & Appetizers 40
Eggs 54
Soups 56
Breads & Baked Delicacies 64
Stuffed Foods & Croquettes 76
Fish 90
Meat & Poultry 102
Desserts 120

Additional Recipes 128
Index 132

Part One: Food in Israel

The arrival of immigrants from around the globe has produced a diverse yet distinctive national cuisine

Israelis seem to have an insatiable appetite for life. Passionate, affable, rambunctious, they are among the world's most welcoming and hospitable people. The casual observer might say that their zest for life and pride in their country stems from a long and enduring history. Indeed, there are three thousand years of tradition woven into Israel's cultural identity and this has resulted in a remarkably wide variety of culinary offerings.

Nowhere is the Israeli passion for life more pronounced than around their food tables at home and in their restaurants—Israelis love to entertain, whether other members of their family or visiting guests. Almost every holiday is celebrated with food, though dishes can vary greatly from household to household. Israelis of Polish heritage, for instance, celebrate the same Hanukah or Passover as those of Bukharan ancestry—or indeed Indian or American—but with a very different spread.

Apart from its long history, what is most notable about Israeli cuisine is the dramatic change that has come over it in the last one hundred years. The multicultural influx of Jews from all over the world—from Eastern Europe, the Mediterranean, Russia, and Africa—has led to a diverse infusion of previously unknown foods and cooking techniques. People from as many as seventy different cultures have converged on Israel to create this distinctive and diverse cuisine.

The State of Israel—a small country of 15,000 square miles (only slightly larger than the state of Massachusetts, USA)—was created in a hostile environment and, until recently, remained under a constant threat of war. In keeping with its enduring struggles through history, the nascent state maintained a cuisine of bare simplicity—produce, breads, and locally raised meats, seasoned with local spices—an ethos that has prevailed until quite recently. Only in the last few decades have Israelis become significantly more extravagant in their eating habits, perhaps to compensate for all those years of austerity.

Today, many Israelis savor caviar from the Caspian Sea, smoked salmon from Norway, prime tuna from Japan, as well as imported oysters and lobsters. They drink fine Bordeaux and Burgundy wines from France, and dress salads with balsamic vinegar from Italy.

The combination of recent innovations blended into the existing local Arab diet, which continues to be a staple element of the Israeli kitchen, and a long history spanning several thousand years, has led to a gradual evolution of an Israeli cuisine that respects both local as well as imported produce and tastes.

Page 2:
The 12th century Byzantine Church of the Transfiguration sits atop Mount Tabor in Israel's Jezreel Valley. Christain tradition has it that this was the place where Moses and Elijah appeared before Jesus and his three disciples, Peter, John, and James.

Opposite:
A spread of Arab meze at the American Colony Hotel, formerly a Pasha's palace that was built in the 19th century.

Three Thousand Years of Culinary History

*From King Solomon's table to the birth
of a glorious new nation*

If it can be said that a country has a collective culinary memory, Israel's consists of foods and cooking methods that span three thousand years of history. Over that time period, Israeli cuisine has been influenced and shaped by cultures throughout Asia, Africa and Europe. Exactly how this tiny country became such a culinary melting pot is irrevocably tied to its religious and ethnic history.

Records provide insight into the culinary life of the region in the days of the kings of ancient Israel, as far back as 968 BC. The table of King Solomon, who ruled for forty years, seems to have been remarkably advanced for its time. Solomon feasted on legs of roasted partridge; fattened goose liver; lentil stew prepared with bone marrow, onions, garlic, and coriander; and spicy red wine. These foods were succulently prepared for the king and his courtiers, though the vast majority of the people in his time lived on a much simpler diet.

Following the destruction of the First Temple (which Solomon built in 950 BC) and the rebuilding of the Second Temple in 516 BC, Alexander the Great brought his Hellenistic influence to Israel. Soon after, Roman culture also held sway as Pompey, the Roman general, annexed the region as a Roman province in 63 BC. Of course, these series of events took more then four hundred years to unfold, but Hellenistic and Roman culture came to inspire heavily the manners and cuisine of the priests and nobility of Jerusalem. For instance, the ability to hire a professional chef became the highest mark of social status. Guests received written invitations to parties and were welcomed with a few piquant dishes and an alcoholic drink to whet the appetite. They were then offered pickled fish and smoked meat, fried eggs and honey, accompanied by pickled vegetables, olives, radishes, celery, lettuce or cucumbers, and tart or very sweet fruits.

The food of Palestine, as the Romans named it, or the Holy Land, as it became generally known throughout the Christian world, was the same as that of the surrounding Middle Eastern countries. Home-grown diets were enhanced by imported spices and herbs, easily accessible because of the land's position at the crossroads of east-west trade routes. The people of Israel shared the land and its produce with many other nations. In addition to what they grew locally, the inhabitants also ate the meat of animals that foraged in the scrub of the land. With the rise of the Islamic faith in the seventh century, the religious prohibitions of both Muslims and Jews meant that no pork was consumed; instead the people subsisted on the meat of mountain goats and sheep.

There is little else known about the food of the Holy Land until the tenth century, when the Muslim geographer Al-Mukadasi wrote of clean and organized markets selling food in Jerusalem. He mentions quince, raisins, bananas, oranges, cheese, pine nuts, and honey. Bananas arrived from India, causing great astonishment, as indicated in this description by a visitor as late as 1280: "They have a thick peel like a pea pod, but the color is a shade of light yellow. The peel should be disposed of, the fruit inside taken and eaten. Its taste is very sweet, like a delicate butter with honey. ... The fruit has no seeds, and can be totally consumed."

The Crusaders, who invaded from Europe at the end of the eleventh century, were convinced that the banana came from the Garden of Eden.

This scene from Genesis 18:8 depicts Abraham as he serves three men cheese curds, milk and roasted meat under a terebinth tree while his servant washes their feet. The three men were two angels and the Lord, appearing as a theophany.

Indeed, they were taken by much of the local cuisine, which by now included foods from the Persian nobility and the courts of the Muslim khalifs in Baghdad, both of whom had arrived with their cuisines several hundred years earlier. The Crusaders liked the Middle Eastern spices, and especially the wine that had been banned during

Muslim rule. In a burst of creativity, they brought snow from the mountains of Lebanon and doused it with wine to make summer coolers, or they infused it with fruit juices to create sweet sherbets.

In the sixteenth century Turkish provincial cuisine became dominant following the Ottoman conquest of the Holy Land. The Ottomans brought

The ancient port of Jaffa, now a suburb of Tel Aviv, is believed to have been operating for four thousand years.

visited in the mid-nineteenth century, chronicled their visit to a typical harem. At the time, their writing provided a fascinating study of table etiquette in an environment of privilege that would have rivaled that of King Solomon.

"After coffee, small low inlaid mother-of-pearl tables were brought in. On them were placed large brass trays with a huge and rich variety of small dishes filled with an assortment of foods. ... Flat pita breads, either halved or whole, were used to wipe the plate and bring the food to one's mouth. The cooked food was cut ahead of time, which enabled us to eat without cutlery ... they presented large wooden spoons for the soup and sherbet, on which they sprinkled rose water. Every guest received an embroidered napkin ... to wipe her hands and protect her clothes."

No doubt, the Western visitors also dined on sweets, an inseparable part of every meal at that time. Specialties included the pistachio and honeyed *baklava*, the semolina-based *knafeh*, *rakhat lakum* (the local version of Turkish delight), marzipans, sugared nuts, almonds, and different kinds of *halvah*.

with them dramatic new ways of cooking. They combined meat with yogurt and prepared barbecued *shashlik* and kebab. The practice of stuffing certain foods, such as vine leaves, zucchini, and eggplant, quickly grew in popularity, and tomatoes and potatoes arrived from the New World via Europe.

Some travelers arriving in Israel from the west in the nineteenth century wrote admiringly of the local cuisine. An Italian princess, Cristina di Belgiojoso, and a Madam Sara Berkley Johnson, who

Jewish immigration began anew in the late nineteenth century, and with it came a whole array of foods. The next fifty years witnessed the return of a people who had been exiled from their homeland for almost two thousand years. Having absorbed the eating customs of the communities into which they had wandered (whilst, of course, maintaining their own traditions and prohibitions), the Jews brought their acquired tastes back to their roots and their own ancient culture.

Jewish immigrants arriving from central Europe continued to eat their favorite foods, such as *schnitzels* and *strudels*, while Russian Jews clung to their *tchai* and *borscht*. The immigrants came from all over, offering a homecoming gift of endless cuisine from the farthest reaches of the world.

At the same time, the occupying forces of the British mandate, which began after World War I, brought yet another set of eating habits to Israel. During the period of British rule, salons across the region offered cocktail hour, replete with crystal service. Five o'clock tea was served regularly, accompanied by finger sandwiches and sweets. However, with the end of the mandate, and the birth of the State of Israel in 1948, these traditions ceased to play any significant role.

Food was extremely basic in the early years of the Israeli state. As in most pioneer societies, preparation of good and sensual food was viewed with some contempt. It was considered more appropriate to save one's time and strength to help build the country. Even at the end of the 1970s, eating habits were still heavily influenced by the spartan rigidity that had marked early Israeli

Two young immigrant girls of Eastern European or Russian origin arrive in Israel at the turn of the twentieth century.

society following the Holocaust.

But people still indulged in the barbecue; its pungent charcoal odors of beef and chicken would linger over the entire country, especially during Independence Day celebrations in May.

It is a method that harkens back to the most basic cooking principles used even before the time of King Solomon and acts as a reminder to all of the long history shared by the peoples of this land.

The Land of Milk and Honey

*Seven ancient foods still play a crucial role
in Israeli cuisine*

The Bible often refers to Israel as "the land of milk and honey," a place where countless types of food are plentiful. Israel's varied climate and geography lends itself easily to such a perception even today. Much of Israel enjoys a typically Mediterranean climate. Hot, dry summers are followed by mild, rainy winters. Still, in various pockets of this small country, the climate shifts. Coastal and desert areas tend to be warmer; hilly territories cooler. Soil qualities also differ throughout. With such climatic variety, Israel's location has, for thousands of years, been instrumental in providing its inhabitants with a bounty of foods. Its cuisine is essentially the same as much of the Mediterranean, but is tempered by the country's borders with the Syrian and Arabian deserts to the east, the Sinai Peninsula to the south, and Lebanon to the north.

Seven ingredients emerge from this geographic and climatic mix as the most beloved and the most blessed in Israel. Many believe they are the foundation on which Israeli cuisine rests. They are

loosely known as the seven spices: olives, figs, dates, pomegranates, wheat, barley, and grapes.

Most Mediterranean cuisines are rich with olives and Israel's is no exception. The olive tree is one of the greatest ancient plants of the world. Researchers believe that the fruit of the wild olive tree served as food for primitive man. And, of course, its religious symbolism is well known, as a dove delivered the olive branch to Noah as a first sign of the world's renewal.

Cultivation of the oil presumably began with the development of human cultures. For hundreds of years, olive oil was the main fuel used for lighting. And in religious ceremonies, it was of great importance as an anointing agent, reinforcing its significance during ancient times.

The steady sunlight of the Mediterranean climate is also perfect for the growth of fig trees, so they too have become a mainstay of the Israeli diet. In primitive and ancient societies with a limited supply of sugar, figs helped to preserve cooked fruits. The fig itself is not actually a fruit in the

Opposite and left: Women harvest olives in Galilee. Olives cannot be eaten directly off the branch but require processing to remove the bitterness. A symbol of peace and wisdom, olives have been important for thousands of years as a source of food, oil, fuel and medicinal remedies.

botanical sense of the word, rather a fleshy receptacle containing a large number of small brittle seed-like achenes which are actually the fruits. However, one could surmise that their popularity goes beyond the climatic and the pragmatic. Its tree, after all, is the first to be mentioned in the Bible. Adam and Eve, upon seeing their nakedness, "sewed fig leaves together and made themselves aprons." Thus, for many, the fig is symbolic of knowledge. And in some Arab cultures, its countless seed-like fruits signify fertility.

Dates contain as much natural sugar as figs, so they are often used to sweeten desserts. But they might also add a sweet flavor to vegetable dishes and meat and fish dishes. Throughout history, their preparation has varied. To experience them at their absolute freshest, they can be eaten straight off a bunch. Or, they'll stay preserved in their own natural sugars. They can also be dried, ground into meal, and added to a cake mix, or made into a nice compote for dessert.

The sour taste of the pomegranate is refreshing to those living in the warm climes of Israel. Pomegranates are also taken to represent the universality of understanding and knowledge. This could be tied closely to the beliefs of the ancients, who thought immortality was in store for the man who tasted the pomegranate, so long as he believed in

love. Today, its seeds are used to complement couscous or salads. And sour pomegranates can be concentrated into a syrup for sweet-and-sour dishes.

Many researchers credit the cultivation of wheat and barley with the development of civilized societies. With the grains' discovery, nomads settled down to an existence of hunting, gathering, and farming. Archaeological evidence in Jericho suggests that a village was built near a wheat field as early as 10,000 BC. And barley and wheat were grown along nearby riverbanks until 7,000 BC.

Barley is well-adapted to growing conditions in the Palestine region. In fact, it's a hearty grain all around, adapting well to many climates. Today, wheat is used to make couscous, bulgur (a more refined couscous, also known as burghul), pita bread, and wheat dough for pastries. Barley is also added to *cholent* and other stews.

The popularity of the grape throughout Israel's history is illustrated by rituals and artifacts. Wine is traditionally sipped on the Sabbath, on Jewish holidays and at special ceremonies. Ancient wine cisterns and utensils suggest that this may have been the case for thousands of years. Recently, Israeli wine has greatly improved in quality, due to better strains of grape and better growing areas such as the the Carmel mountain range, the Galilee region, and the Golan heights.

Religion and Food in the Holy Land

On Yom Kippur, Ramadan
and breaking fasts

The land of Israel is the land of the Bible, where the belief in monotheism, and the notion that one God oversees all, emerged. It is the birthplace of Judaism and Christianity, and later it also became holy to Islam. Religion continues to have enormous power and impact on the lives of individuals, and society. And it has also, throughout Israel's long history, had a significant impact on food.

At no time is this more evident than during the rare occasion when the Jewish Passover, Christian Easter, and Islamic festival of sacrifice all fall in the same week. As one would expect, the price of lamb goes up considerably, but something else rises throughout Israel. The noisy clatter of plates and cutlery can be heard from households of each faith, its din intermingling with one another in the air, creating a harmonious sense of peace and unity.

Examples of a shared religious culinary life are numerous. According to the Jewish religion, *matzot* cannot be eaten before the first night of Passover. A humorous passage from the *Jerusalem Talmud* comments on the patience sometimes required for this restriction: "One who eats unleavened bread on Passover eve, is like one who has intercourse with his betrothed in his in-laws' (father-in-law's) house ...". "Wait a little!" is the *Talmud*'s message. And, indeed, Orthodox Jews do wait, as a reminder of the Jews who were hurried into exile from Egypt so quickly that their dough did not have time to rise.

The restriction led to some culinary cooperation many years ago, when Jews and Arabs lived happily side by side. The Jews baked *matzot* in preparation for Passover and the tempting smell spread throughout the city. But since they weren't permitted to eat them just yet, they honored their Arab neighbors with the first and freshest batch. In return, on the evening of the seventh day, when bread was again allowed, the Arabs would bake warm pitas and roast chickpeas, arrange them nicely on a tray, and serve them to their Jewish neighbors. They blessed each other by saying "*sintak chudra!*" meaning "green year!"

Opposite:
A family of Jews from Bukhoro, Uzbekistan.
Left:
Three generations of women from a family of Moroccan origins prepares an elaborate meal featuring couscous.

The prohibition against flour on Passover has led the Jews to develop foods which were made of matza meal or potato flour with ground nuts. A large variety of foods that mix vegetables and milk products have emerged from the more general prohibitions—the dietary laws known as *kashrut*—against eating meat with milk. And because the Sabbath forbade work and burning a fire, a demand arose for recipes that cook slowly over a longer period of time. Chamin, a hearty rich stew, would be prepared on Friday and left to cook overnight to be served as a midday meal on Saturday. The traditional *chamin* consists of meat, potato, barley, and beans, but the recipe varies considerably depending on each groups' traditions.

Common abstinences exist in both the Jewish and Islamic faiths. Both religions, for instance, observe the practice of fasting. Yom Kippur—the Day of Atonement, when people fast and pray for the atonement of their sins, resolve differences with others, pay emotional debts, or donate to charities—is predominant in Judaism. Ramadan—when Muslims pay tribute to Allah and Mohammed through sacrifice, humility, and

Jewish religious prohibitions—those against lighting fire on the Sabbath, mixing meat and milk, eating seafood or pork, and eating leavened bread during Passover—have led to the development of unique foods in Israel and throughout the whole world. Similarly, prohibitions in Islam—those against eating pork, or drinking or cooking with alcohol—have also resulted in special and unique foods.

suppression of all fleshly appetites—occurs once a year in the Islamic faith. Yom Kippur lasts for just one day, whereas the prohibitions of Ramadan are observed between sunrise and sunset every day for a full month.

Breaking the fast can be as full of ritual as the fast itself. On Yom Kippur, the Jews wait for the evening, count three stars in the sky, and drink a sweet beverage. Families who came to Israel from the Balkans break the fast with a white, sweet, cold drink called *pipitada*, which is prepared from melon seeds with sugar and rosewater extract. This drink soothes the empty stomach and its white color symbolizes the purity following the prayers.

Moroccan Jews drink coffee with milk accompanied by an egg beaten with sugar. The egg soothes the throat, which is sore from a long day of praying. Iraqi Jews eat a compote made of quince while others drink fresh pomegranate juice or hot milk with some cardamom.

The Samaritans, from the ancient city of Samaria in neighboring Jordan, eat a compote made of dried apricot and pomegranate. The Ashkenazi families, those from Russia, Poland, and Eastern Europe, break the fast by drinking strong coffee with honey or cinnamon cake and then an alcoholic drink—cognac, arak, or whisky—accompanied by herring.

Muslims break their fasts every day at sunset. In typical practice, the thunder of gunshots would announce the end of a fasting day. The fast is broken with a small dish, usually sweet, to overcome weakness. It usually consists of a fig or a date, and the people drink something sweet, such as *tamarhindi* or almond milk, to soothe the stomach.

The liberation from religious authority has resulted in a large segment of society being unaware of many of the kosher laws and the practices surrounding religious observances. Many think that the *kashrut* limitations and other prohibitions dictated by religion leave one with a lower quality of food. Others believe that, through the traditions inherent in religious observance, cooking fundamentals from three thousand years ago can be touched and honored. Today, Israeli cuisine has imposed a whole new set of culinary standards on what used to be considered basic, simple foods.

Opposite:
A Yemenite Jewish bride and groom, together with their families, celebrate the Hina ceremony, held one week before the actual wedding. The ancient Hina ceremony, recently revived among Israeli Jews, celebrates the use of henna, a reddish-brown dye, to paint the palms of the bride and, in times past, to scare away demons.
Left:
Two young dairy workers—Ethiopian Jews newly arrived in Israel—carry sacks full of fermented milk, the first stage before it turns to white cheese.

Markets and Street Food

The fruits of an ancient agriculture may still be experienced through its local vendors

Markets are an integral part of life in Israel. The more exacting cooks know that the best produce merchant, the best butcher, or the best delicatessen cannot substitute for the role of the open market. Not only will you find the essence of Israel's cuisine in its markets, but you will learn about the Israeli people and their land.

In Jerusalem, the network of markets in the old city started long before the time of the Crusaders, more than 700 years ago. Browsing from the butcher's market to the oil-press, and through the chicken and herb markets, smells of herbs mingle with incense, which is burnt by the merchants selling souvenirs. Women farmers sit on the ground dressed in colorful garments, selling huge cauliflowers and other vegetables.

At the butcher's market, salads are prepared with a large butcher's knife and delivered across the alley to diners at a restaurant. Farther along, across from the egg and sheep cheese pickled in salted water, a stallholder stands behind a mortar preparing his

legendary hummus. Just beyond, oranges hailing from Jericho, grapes from Hebron, huge yellow lemons, and guavas with delightfully lingering odors, beckon.

A highlight of the Jerusalem markets is the delicious *mutabek*—a thin, brittle pastry filled with salted sheep cheese in a sugar syrup- made by Zalatimo, located behind the Church of the Holy Sepulcher. The Jaafar (the oil-press market), where you can get the famous *knafeh* (thin red dough, filled with salted sheep cheese and dipped in syrup spiced with rose water), also shouldn't be overlooked. And from the moving carts, it is worthwhile to taste the sesame pretzels that come with a little bag of *za'atar* for dipping.

Wandering beverage sellers make their rounds in the market holding trays full of glasses. Others ring bells while carrying a metal jug on their back, shiny and adorned with plastic flowers, containing *sus* or *tamarhindi* beverages. Outside Damascus Gate, at El-Arz beverage store, you can sample

Opposite:
Red paprika is piled high, ready to be weighed out at this spice stall in Lewinsky market.
Left:
A Yemenite Jew shops for fresh fruit and vegetables at the market of Rosh Haayin.

A wide variety of fresh vegetables is available from the Hacarmel market in Tel Aviv.

means "alcohol" in Arabic), which are the markets' pubs. Since they open and close sporadically, and move around often, the usual way of finding them is to ask around in the market itself. Nearby, stop at Azura's to sample some authentic Iraqi cuisine, like *kibbeh*, seasoned ground meat deep-fried in a jacket of bulgur, or cracked wheat.

Some of the more interesting markets are the ones that move around, the mobile markets. This network began with the markets of Ramleh and Lod. The former serves up a Tunisian sandwich that includes a spicy Torshi sauce made of pumpkin, tuna, pickled lemons, eggs, potatoes, and salad. Sample the famous Ramleh lemonade, made of real lemons that are ground with their peel; it's known for evoking thirst rather than quenching it. High quality paprika from the Zeitan village is also available only in this market and the Lod market. Ramleh Market also stops in Netanya, Kiryat Malachi, Ashdod, Beer-Sheba, and Rosh-Ha'ayeen, but is always known by the same name.

The Lod Market (open Tuesdays) belongs to the true cooks—determined women who would not

almond milk. This delicious beverage soothes the stomach and has been called Heaven's Wine.

The Machaneh Yehudah market, in the western part of the Holy City, was founded during the Ottoman period, when Arabs from the nearby areas came to west Jerusalem to sell their merchandise. Today, it symbolizes the essence of the authentic Jerusalem experience. Here, you may find little restaurants, or *hamarot* ("hamar" dream of allowing a tomato or bean enter their kitchen unless they themselves have first checked it thoroughly. At the Lod Market, you will not find new cuisine vegetables, such as endive, curly lettuce, or asparagus. Instead, its tables overflow with traditional black eggplant, real red peppers, green Colombian coffee, artichoke thorns, vine leaves, and homemade filo leaves.

In Ashdod, one of Israel's busiest ports, the market is based at the seashore, and its character is Mediterranean, even colorfully North African. The blue sea beyond, and the countless ships and boats moored at the docks, brings this market to life.

In the old city of Akko, also on the Mediterranean, more varied goods can be found because of its diverse inhabitants: Jewish immigrants from North Africa, Russia, Romania, and Poland, as well as new Arab immigrants and others. This permanent market is reputed for its high quality wares. In fact, the best hummus in the market hails from Said's. It's said that he stirs his hummus so vigorously that his hands can hardly be seen. You can also find a superb *knafeh* here, and for dessert, sip a lemonade with rose-water. The market at Akko

A spice vendor displays his wares at Rosh Haayin market.

is also the place to purchase some of the best quality herbs, spices, and fish.

Whether mobile or permanent, Israel's markets are a feast for the senses. And because they come directly from the fields, bypassing wholesalers, they provide the freshest and best produce. Add to this the vibrancy of local color, smell and personalities and the whole experience becomes a celebration of the senses.

The New Israeli Cuisine

Bold chefs forge a new culinary direction for their nation

Though the roots of Israel stretch back more than three thousand years, the nation itself has enjoyed independence for a little over fifty years. Thus, even when we talk about an ancient people, a purely Israeli cuisine—one that is based on long and enduring traditions—hasn't had the chance to fully mature. Yet, the cuisine that exists in Israel today is eclectic and interesting. Not only has it evolved from the contributions of countless non-indigenous cultures the world over, it has also addressed the demands of second-generation Israelis who are leaving behind culinary traditions of the Old World while simultaneously severing ties to the history of the Diaspora.

In the 1970s, restaurants serving Chinese, Italian, French, and Japanese food brought the world's aromas to Israel. More recently, fusion cuisine has made its presence felt in some daring establish-ments—accompanied by exciting décor and high standards of professional service—combining different styles and sophisticated techniques to create new culinary experiences.

Israelis, therefore, seem to live a double culinary life. Regardless of their origin, they eat Jewish ethnic food that connects them to their cultural roots, and in the evening they visit a restaurant to sample sushi or *paté de foie gras*—accompanied by wine—so they can feel a part of the larger world.

Until recently, being a cook was not a desire of the young Israeli. Cooks were considered an untalented class of people who would be stationed in the military base kitchen because they weren't capable of anything else. Today, Israelis attend world culinary schools in France, Italy, and the United States. The improved status of the profession has made it a legitimate career. The nineties was a

Opposite:
Top-notch Israeli restaurants, such as Ocean in Jerusalem, are comparable to the finest found anywhere.
Right:
(from left to right) Haim Cohen, Israel Aharoni and Eyal Shani are three of Israel's most prominent chefs.

decade of varied and rich culinary creations, with a concerted attempt to create a quality cuisine that maximizes local input to yield very exciting results.

Eyal Shani, one of Israel's most talented seafood chefs, is among a group of enthusiastic chefs leading the way. He served a carpaccio of sea bass long before sashimi and its Spanish cousin, *costiza*, arrived in the country. He made it with sea grouper, sliced razor thin and marinated with lemon juice, olive oil, and coarse sea salt. Adding more international flair, he added hot Japanese wasabi sauce.

Combining past and present with a most appealing flavor, Moise Peer features a delectable goose-liver appetizer in his elegant Mishkenot Shaananim restaurant, overlooking Jerusalem's Old City. This successful marriage of an unlikely couple successfully combines figs, one of the seven spices of Israel that has grown in Jerusalem for 6,000 years, and the fattened goose liver, a more recent product. It's topped off with a sweet sauce.

Chef Israeli Aharoni returned home from traveling the world some twenty years ago and opened his first restaurant in Tel Aviv, changing the gastronomic tastes of Israel. With a great love of knowledge and food, combined with prodigious talent, he has whipped up more than fifteen best-selling cookbooks plus a weekly column in a leading Israeli newspaper. His restaurant, Tapuach Zahav (The Golden Apple) has been his crowning achievement to date but with its recent closure, patrons are eagerly awaiting his next venture.

Tamar Bly and Ezra Kedem, the owners and chefs of Arcadia in Jerusalem, have made their restaurant one of Israel's best, with their use of fresh local herbs, fruits and vegetables from the open Machaneh Yehudah market. They delicately work their ingredients into a fusion of Italian- and French-inspired cuisine that's always surprising and exciting.

Haim Cohen and Irit Shenkar created their restaurant Keren out of a small wooden building that once resided in the state of Maine in the United States. The house's history is no less intriguing than the recipes they create inside. It was brought to Jaffa by 157 American colonists in 1866, but they were driven out by the local Turkish community. After seeing many owners, including the Germans and British, Cohen and Shenkar saw its potential as their dream restaurant. Today, they cook up chickpea soup with squid and parmesan cheese, a dish the American colonists could never have imagined.

In Jerusalem, mother and daughter cook up some nostalgia for their loyal clientele of Sephardic Jews. At Daniella Sofer's restaurant called Barud, the owner and her mother, Simcha, prepare *pastels* that harken back to days in Spain before many Sephardic Jews returned to Israel. Pastel, in the Spanish Jewish dialect Ladino, means "stuffed dough." Pastelikos are small stuffed pastries, the pride of Sephardic Jewish cooks. The varieties of dough, shapes, and fillings are endless, ranging from the *burekas* of Turkey and the Balkans to the pastels of the Jewish community from Salonika, Greece. The local Palestinian community also has its stuffed pastries, such as a *sambusak* of stuffed filo leaves.

Barud proves that—even in a region bursting with haute cuisine—there's still plenty of room for traditional eateries.

Part Two: The Israeli Kitchen

Modern appliances and traditional implements stand side by side in Israeli kitchens

It's been said that, if an Israeli invites you to his home for dinner, the invitation is from the heart. Certainly, Israelis are known the world over for their hospitality. And one might surmise that the source of their kindness is a long family tradition. For Israeli culture, straddling thousands of years, has been built on its human relationships as much as on its religious and political history. It would, then, be unthinkable for anyone to decline an Israeli's invitation into his or her kitchen.

Of course, what you find in the kitchen depends on many factors. After all, methods of food preparation arrived from every corner of the world to give birth to what is today known as Israeli cuisine. Ashkenazi Jewish culinary traditions arrived here from Eastern Europe and Russia; Sephardic Jewish traditions came from other Mediterranean countries—from Iberia to Africa. Other cuisines were brought here from Austria, the Balkans, and Turkey. Jews and other immigrants have come from more than seventy countries to make Israel their home. Just as Israel's culture consists of myriad ethnicities, so have its cuisine and culinary methods been shaped by various traditions.

Ashkenazi Jewish tradition recalls the communal bakehouse. In medieval Eastern Europe, where Jews of the 19th century had formed their own distinct communities, or shtetls, cooking facilities at home were rare, so housewives carried their food to be cooked in a communal oven. The local congregation provided copper cauldrons and wooden cooking utensils for their use. Cholent, or *chamin*—traditionally a stew of meat, potatoes, beans, and grain—was cooked at the bakehouse overnight Friday. Because the Sabbath prohibited work after sunset Friday and into Saturday, housewives prepared the stew in a large pot on Friday, sealed the lid with a flour and water paste, and walked it to the communal oven. The seal fulfilled two purposes, one culinary and one quirky: it cooked the stew under pressure and, according to some, it ensured that no one would add any undesirable ingredients to your meal.

The name *cholent* is believed to have come from the medieval French *chaud* (hot) and *lent* (slow), and it helped to perpetuate a long tradition of slow cooking. If prepared in today's home kitchen, *cholent* is still cooked slowly overnight. Use a heavy

Opposite:
Israeli kitchens today feature both modern and traditional appliances with which to prepare such dishes as Cholent.
Left.
A traditional kerosene stove known as a ptiliya.

pot or casserole dish in a low oven. A tightly fitting lid will suffice instead of the flour and water seal. Not all Israelis today have the patience for such protracted preparation; *cholent* can now be purchased pre-cooked in the frozen section of a market.

The labor-intensive nature of *cholent* preparation was typical of Jewish culinary tradition, in which food preparation was a labor of love for one's family and one's faith. Kugel, or egg noodles, was also made from scratch. The dough was kneaded, flattened on a floured sheet, rolled into a cylinder, and sliced thin. The resulting ribbons were set out to dry. Though cumbersome when held up to today's conveniences, this technique remains the preference of customary cooks who choose to forgo the modern-day pasta maker.

Sephardic Jewish tradition has contributed more lively fare to the tables of Israel, along the lines of King Solomon's table. In Song of Songs, there is a description of a banquet of fruit, herbs, spices, flower essences, and colors typical of Mediterranean cuisine. But the braising and stewing seen in the preparation of *cholent* is equally common in the Sephardic tradition.

Cooking fats of the past tended to be heavy. Alya, the fat from a sheep's or lamb's tail, was popular as a staple, and it is still used by some today, although ordinary butter or margarine is generally preferred. But *samna*, a clarified butter commonly made from buffalo's milk, is considered the best option. To clarify it, the butter is melted over boiling water and strained through a thin, dampened muslin sheet. The impurities that cause butter to burn are thus eliminated and the resulting *samna* is rich and strong. In fact, it's best to use less *samna* where you might otherwise use a lot of butter. One type of *samna*, ghee, is readily available in specialty stores.

Another staple, couscous, was introduced by immigrants from Morocco. The grain is commonly served with chicken or lamb. It is best prepared from scratch with a couscousiere: a form of steamer pot, comprising two compartments, which cooks the grains over boiling water. A colander placed over a simple saucepan will also suffice.

Other useful implements in the Israeli kitchen include a corer, with which to remove pulp from zucchini and eggplant, a garlic press, a grater for grating cheeses and vegetables, a meat grinder or food processor, and skewers for kebabs. A mortar and pestle also come in handy. The wooden, metal, or porcelain bowl serves as a confining vessel in which to crush garlic and spices with the rounded hammer. Many might prefer a rolling pin or blender, but devoted cooks claim that there is absolutely no sufficient substitute for the mortar and pestle.

Another component of the Israeli diet that should not be compromised is coffee. The preferred blend, Turkish coffee, is best prepared using the *finjan*. This open-topped metal pot with a long handle is used on a stovetop, but a small saucepan can easily achieve similar results.

Israeli Ingredients

*Preparing authentic Israeli cuisine is simple
once you know the basic ingredients*

ALLSPICE: Named from the supposed resemblance of its hot aromatic smell and taste to that of combined cinnamon, cloves, and nutmeg. Allspice is actually the dried, unripened berry of a West Indian tree, *Pimenta dioica*. Allspice became popular as a seasoning in Europe in the seventeenth century and is therefore a relatively recent import to the Israeli cuisine.

ARAK: This Eastern Mediterranean spirit is distilled from sugar beet or grains and flavored with aniseed and herbs. It is used sparingly in Israeli cuisine and can be substituted with Greek Ouzo.

BAHAR OF AMBAH: This is a yellow mixture that includes turmeric, ground fenugreek, spicy paprika, allspice, and ground cardamom. Some add other spices such as ground ginger, a tad of ground cloves, or ground nutmeg. Ambah is used for seasoning picante mixtures of pickled vegetables. The *ambah* sauce is served as a sauce for meats in pita such as *shwarmah*.

BAHAR MEAT SPICE MIXTURE: This dark mixture of herbs includes black pepper, allspice, ground cloves, ground ginger, ground cinnamon, and nutmeg. Some add a pinch of ground cardamom seeds. It is primarily used to season grilled meat, ground meat mixtures for fillings, kebab, and cutlets.

BULGUR: Bulgur is the Turkish word for cracked wheat; it is also commonly known by its Arabic name, Burghul. Cracked wheat dishes are the pride of the Lebanese, Syrians, Druze, and the Galilee Arabs. It is the primary ingredient in Tabouleh, and crushed with lamb meat to make Kibbeh Naaya, or with Stuffed Kibbeh.

CAPERS: The caper bush grows wild in many parts of Israel, especially in rock crevices and on stone walls. From the caper bush comes the caper berry. After capers have been pickled in salt or vinegar to remove their bitterness, they add a special flavor to herring salad, roasted red peppers, potato salad, smoked salmon, cheeses, spreads, sandwiches, warm and cold fish sauces, chickens, pasta, and bran.

CHALLAH: Challah is a loaf of white bread containing eggs, and leavened with yeast. The bread is often formed into braided loaves and glazed with egg before baking. Challah is traditionally eaten by Jews on the Sabbath, and on ceremonial occasions.

CINNAMON: Four thousand years ago, cinnamon was brought from China and South Asia through Indonesia to Madagascar via small boats, creating a trade route called "the cinnamon path." From Madagascar, cinnamon was transferred

Bulgur

Capers

Fenugreek

Green Almonds

Horse Radish

Mint

Paprika

north to the Nile valley, and thence to Israel. The Arabs season their meat and chicken with cinnamon that has a spicy sweet aroma, and mix it with nuts for pastry fillings which are then dipped in sugar syrup. The Jews use cinnamon to season their cakes and cookies, carrot dishes, baked fruits, fruit compotes, and hot beverages such as *sachlav* and tea.

FENNEL: Fennel seeds are always included in pickling spices, added to cucumbers, olives, and even herring. You can use them to add flavor to bread, salted cookies, beverages, fish marinades, sausages, cabbage dishes, and soups. Fennel seeds can also be used in the water of cooked artichokes, potatoes, or fish, with wonderful results. An infusion of fennel reportedly helps subdue stomach aches, and the stems can be added to hot charcoal or underneath meats and fish when grilling or roasting. The fennel leaves, which are similar to dill leaves, can be put in a fresh salad or in any other dish. They can also be added to mayonnaise, soup, vinaigrette sauces, pasta, and roasted fish.

FENUGREEK: Fenugreek seeds are used by the Yemenite Jews primarily in preparing the fenugreek sauces that accompany pastries and soups. In the spring the Arab farmers gather the young branches of the plant and prepare a salad, or season the fenugreek with refined butter.

FIG: The fig tree and its fruit are symbolic of fertility. Prepared fresh or dried, it is used in jams, syrup, honey and alcohol. Dried figs were once used as coffee and tobacco substitutes. Fresh figs should be bought when they are ripe, juicy, and soft; check their ripeness by pressing lightly on them. They should have a strong sweet smell, a fresh color, and an unblemished skin. If they smell sour, you know that they are not fresh. Figs are delicious halved with few drops of Ouzo or lemon juice on them or stuffed with goat cheese, or ground nuts, and served with ice cream, fruit sauce, sour or whipped cream, or vanilla.

GREEN ALMONDS: Green almonds are unripe almonds, enjoyed at the stage before the shell and inner brown peel has developed. Green almonds can be eaten whole, along with its thick green peel. They give a fresh sour taste and a verdant aroma. Green almonds can be pickled or scalded in salt water and served in a vinaigrette sauce. You may add green almonds to meat or chicken dishes and even fry them with crushed garlic, chili peppers, and ginger.

GREEN CARDAMOM: Green cardamom is the oldest herb in the world. Originally from India, it is the herb that made Arab coffee so famous. When it arrived in Europe the Greeks and the Romans used it for cologne. In Israel it is used to season ground meat, fish, *s'chug*, honey, cookies, bread, ice cream, jams, and pickles.

HORSERADISH ROOT: Before using, the root of the horseradish should be peeled, grated or minced. If you use a grater it is better to do it in an open area, since the vapors can cause the eyes to tear. After the horseradish has been grated, it loses its spiciness quickly. Therefore, only small quantities should be prepared at a time. The horseradish root is used as bitter herbs for the Seder on Passover, and the horseradish liquid, which accumulates during grating, can be used in sauces, fish, meats, sausages, potato salad, and even as a basis for vinaigrette sauce.

MINT: The mint plant, which always grew wild in Israel, was recognized when the Greeks, Romans, and Arab tribes arrived. Today in Israel, mint is very popular among all ethnic groups—especially in tea, for seasoning fresh vegetable and fruit salads, and dried in all manner of Arabic cuisine. The chopped leaves may be added to stuffed grape leaves, pickled eggplant, or even pasta. The Israeli mint leaves have a different taste to that of European mint; but one kind of mint leaf can easily be substituted for another in recipes.

PAPRIKA: Paprika is the second most popular herb in Israel, after black pepper. It gives a fiery red color to the North African and Hungarian fish dishes, meats, and eggs. Paprika arrived in Israel at the beginning of the sixteenth century along with the tomato, and together the two turned pale dishes into blushing ones.

PINE NUTS: When the seeds in the pinecones ripen, the scales open, and the pine nuts fall to the ground. Shelling pine nuts is difficult; one has to find a way of breaking the hard black peel without marring the white kernel inside. They enrich the flavors of rice, and fresh salads.

POMEGRANATE: When the seeds are added to salads, rice, couscous, stuffing, sauces and beverages, it is impossible not to appreciate the distinctive pomegranate taste, texture, and color. At various beverage stands in Israel, the fresh fruit is squeezed into cups. It is also used in sherbets and sauces. Cooked pomegranates are used for stuffing chicken and cutlets. The best pomegranates are the large ones with a shiny peel, without stains and scratches. They can be stored, without refrigeration, for 2–3 months. If left in the sun, they tend to crack. Where a recipe calls for pomegranate sauce, and a ready-made product is not available, squeeze the juice from fresh pomegranate seeds and reduce it to a syrup.

Pine Nuts

ROSE WATER AND CITRUS EXTRACTS: In keeping with ancient cuisine, these flower extracts are used to season pastries, Middle-Eastern cookies, *rakhat lakum*, candy, cold beverages, and even coffee.

SUMACH: Also known as rhus, sumach is a sour and delicate herb used by Israeli Arabs to season lamb, kebabs, fish, eggs, soup, salads salted pastries, yoghurt, sauces, and vinegar. It can also be used, together with fresh mint, to make a refreshing and sour beveage.

Rose Flowers

TAHINA: Also known as tahini and tehina, tahina is a thick paste made from fresh ground raw sesame seeds, and is a key ingredient in Hummus. Tahina is widely available from specialty stores. It can also be made into a sauce with the addition of lemon juice and various herbs.

ZA'ATAR: The *za'atar* is considered *the* herb of Israel; in Hebrew it is called "Biblical moss." The fresh leaves are baked or fried on pita bread with olive oil, used in salads, or to season soups and goat cheese. Some add the leaves to lamb cuts before roasting, while others add them to shish kebabs. Oregano, thyme and marjoram are cultivated herbs from the same family and can be used as substitutes.

Sumach

Za'atar

Part Three: The Recipes

*Basic recipes for dips, sauces, pickles, and condiments precede
the main recipes, which start on page 40*

Tahina Sauce • *Sesame Seed Sauce*

Also known as tahini or tehina, raw tahina is a thick paste made of crushed sesame seeds that is stirred into Hummus. This recipe for Tahina Sauce is a slightly more liquid adaptation of basic tahina paste and is poured over Falafel (page 44), shashlik, and Kebab (page 116). It is also used to accompany chickpea and dried fava bean dishes, as well as other Arab specialties. Tahina Sauce is also part of a traditional *meze*, served on a dish to be wiped up with warm pita. Tahina Sauce is best if made just prior to serving, but it keeps well in the refrigerator for two to three days (bring to room temperature for at least half an hour before serving).

> 3/4 cup (180 ml) tahina paste (fresh ground
>   sesame paste)
> Juice of 2 medium lemons
> 2–3 cloves garlic, crushed
> Salt to taste
> 2 tablespoons chopped parsley leaves
>   (optional)
> 1 1/2 cups chopped parsley leaves and juice
>   of additional 1/2 lemon (optional)
> *Garnish*: 2–3 tablespoons olive oil

Put the sesame paste into a deep bowl and stir in the lemon juice with a wooden spoon until the mixture lightens in color. Add enough lukewarm water to make a thick, creamy mixture. Add the crushed garlic, salt, and parsley, and mix well. The consistency should be that of a thick dip. For a green Tahina Sauce, add 1 1/2 cups chopped parsley leaves and the juice of another 1/2 lemon. If desired, serve with 2 or 3 tablespoons of fresh olive oil poured over the sauce.

Roasted Tomato Sauce

This sauce is traditionally served with grilled Lamb Kebabs (page 116).

> 4–5 tomatoes
> 2–3 cloves garlic, crushed
> 1/4 cup (60 ml) olive oil
> Salt to taste

Place the tomatoes on a lit grill and roast to blacken on all sides. Peel off the skin, chop finely, and add the garlic, oil, and salt.

Measurements

Measurements in this book are given in both imperial and metric form. For volume measurements, 1 measuring **cup** contains 250 ml (roughly 8 fl oz); 1 **teaspoon** contains 5 ml, while 1 **tablespoon** contains 15 ml or the equivalent of 3 teaspoons. Australian readers please note that the standard Australian tablespoon is larger, containing 20 ml or 4 teaspoons, so use only 3/4 tablespoon when following the recipes.

Opposite:
*Clockwise from
top: Hummus,
fava beans, and
Tahina.*

Yogurt Sauce

As with Roasted Tomato Sauce, Yogurt Sauce is traditionally served with grilled Kebabs (page 116).

> 2 cups (500 ml) plain yogurt (preferably sheep's)
> 1 tablespoon sweet or hot paprika
> 2 tablespoons olive oil

Garnish:
Parsley, chopped fine
Pine nuts (also known as pignolia or pignoli nuts)

In a microwave or on the stove, warm the yogurt—but be careful not to boil. Pour some onto individual plates. Mix the paprika with the oil. Lay grilled Kebabs (page 116) on the plates with the yogurt and sprinkle over some of the paprika mix. Roast the pine nuts in a small pan over medium heat very briefly. Garnish with chopped parsley and roasted pine nuts.

Chrain • *Spicy Horseradish Sauce*

> About 6 oz (180 g) horseradish root, peeled and finely grated (or substitute your favorite bottled brand)
> 4–5 small whole red beets
> $1/2$ cup (125 ml) vinegar or lemon juice
> 1 teaspoon salt
> $1/4$ cup (60 ml) sugar

Place the grated horseradish root in a bowl. Place the beets, along with 1 tablespoon of vinegar or lemon juice, in a pan of water. Bring to a boil and simmer until soft. When soft, allow to cool, peel off the skins, and grind them into the horseradish. Add the remaining vinegar, salt, and sugar.

Zhoug • *Hot Pepper Sauce*

This fragrant hot pepper sauce was brought to Israel by immigrants from Yemen, who add it to all their dishes. It has become one of Israel's most popular condiments. Zhoug adds heat and spice to Falafel (page 44) and to Hummus (page 42). Zhoug is also spread over fish before cooking and added sparingly to sandwiches made with white cheese, eggs, salami, and/or avocado.

> 1 large sprig cilantro (coriander) leaves
> 3–4 fresh green chile peppers with seeds, coarsely chopped
> 3–4 cloves garlic, peeled
> $1/4$ teaspoon ground cumin
> $1/4$ teaspoon ground cloves
> $1/4$ teaspoon ground cardamom
> Salt to taste

Wash the cilantro leaves, and dry them well. Put the cilantro, chopped peppers, and garlic into a food processor and blend. Add the spices and continue to grind to a paste.

Red Zhoug • *Red Hot Pepper Sauce*

> 12 dried red chiles
> 3–7 peeled cloves garlic, according to taste
> Salt to taste

Soak the chiles in water for 2 hours. Drain, then grind with the garlic by hand or in a food processor. Season to taste.

Labaneh • *Sour Yogurt Dressing*

Labaneh is a yogurt-based sour cheese found in Arab markets throughout Israel. It has become so popular that it can also be found in any Israeli supermarket, but it can easily be made from any good organic yogurt.

8 cups (2 litres) yogurt
1 teaspoon salt
Cheesecloth or paper towel

Line a large colander with the cheesecloth or paper towel, making sure it overlaps the colander by a good amount. Mix the yogurt with the salt and pour the mixture into the lined colander. Tie the cheesecloth (or close the paper towel), place the colander over an even bigger bowl into which the mixture can drain.

The Labaneh will be ready in 10 to 12 hours. Transfer it to a dish and cover with olive oil. Place in the refrigerator.

Yogurt Sauce for Stuffed Vine Leaves

1 cup (250 ml) plain yogurt
1 tablespoon chopped mint leaves
1 garlic clove, crushed
1 teaspoon olive oil
Salt to taste

Mix all ingredients and serve chilled.

Pickled Cucumbers

Cucumbers for pickling should be small, young, fresh, firm, and crisp. Pickle them soon after buying, and never pickle cucumbers that have been refrigerated. Pickles are ready to taste four days after being packed into a transparent jar and left under the sun.

6–10 cloves garlic, peeled and halved
  lengthwise
1 green chile pepper, halved
4½ lb (2.25 kg) small young cucumbers
4 dill stalks
Salt
2–3 tablespoons white vinegar
2 bay leaves (optional)
½ teaspoon whole peppercorns (optional)

Wash and sterilize a large pickling jar and lid. Wash the cucumbers well. Place the garlic and green chili pepper at the bottom of the jar. Add the cucumbers and the dill. Measure enough water to cover the cucumbers and transfer the water to a saucepan (without the cucumbers), then add 1 teaspoon salt for each 1 cup (250 ml) water. Add the vinegar, bay leaves, and peppercorns and bring to a boil over a high heat. When the water boils and the salt has dissolved, turn off the heat and allow the liquid to stand for 2–3 minutes before pouring it over the cucumbers. Seal the jar and place under the sun. Leave for 4 days. The cucumbers will have changed color, the bubbling fermentation will have subsided, and the cucumbers will be ready for tasting. Refrigerate immediately.

Pickled Turnips

The freshest turnips are white, with crisp stems. When pickled with the addition of a few slices of beet, they will turn pink.

4$\frac{1}{2}$ lb (2.25 kg) small fresh turnips
1–3 small beets
2$\frac{1}{2}$ teaspoons kosher salt
1 hot green pepper, sliced
3 stalks celery, chopped into 3-in (7-cm) pieces
1$\frac{1}{2}$ cups (375 ml) white vinegar
1 cup (250 ml) water, boiled then chilled

Cut off both ends of the turnips and beets, peel, and slice. Spread the slices in a bowl, sprinkle with salt, mix, and allow to marinate overnight in the refrigerator. The next day, mix in the sliced hot pepper.

Place the chopped celery in a jar large enough to hold all the vegetables and add the sliced turnips, beets, and peppers. Cover the vegtables with the vinegar and the water. The turnips will be ready after 1 or 2 days.

Bahar of Ambah • *Spice Mix for Pickles*

2 teaspoons ground cayenne pepper
2 teaspoons ground turmeric
2 teaspoons ground fenugreek
$\frac{1}{4}$ teaspoon ground allspice
$\frac{1}{4}$ teaspoon ground cardamom
$\frac{1}{4}$ teaspoon ground ginger (optional)
$\frac{1}{4}$ teaspoon ground cloves (optional)
$\frac{1}{4}$ teaspoon of ground nutmeg (optional)

Blend all the spices together. Add the mixture to the brine when making pickles, or rub onto meat prior to cooking. Makes approximately 2$\frac{1}{2}$ tablespoons.

Mixed Pickles

Mixed pickles are like a box of candy for me. Once I start tasting, I cannot stop eating until either my mouth burns or the jar is empty. Actually, once the vinegar and salt are absorbed, the vegetables all taste more or less the same. But each retains its color, shape, and texture. In this recipe the vegetables are gently sautéed before they are pickled. Any combination is possible; a mixture can contain twenty different vegetables, or just two or three. Unripened fruits can also be added—small green plums, green almonds, even unripe grapes.

White vinegar
Water, boiled and cooled
Salt
Corn or sunflower seed oil

For the vegetable mixture, use any or all of the following:

$\frac{1}{2}$ lb (250 g) green beans
3–4 red or green peppers, cut into large pieces
$\frac{1}{2}$ lb (250 g) okra (ladies fingers), stems intact
1 cauliflower, separated into florets, with the stem peeled and finely sliced
3–5 small zucchini (courgettes), cut into thick slices
4–6 carrots, cut diagonally into thick slices
3 unripe pears, cut lengthwise into thick slices
4–5 small eggplants (aubergines), cut into thick slices
2–3 hot green peppers, sliced, deveined and de-seeded
5–7 cloves garlic, peeled and halved
2–3 tablespoons Bahar of Ambah (see recipe)

Prepare a mixture of three parts vinegar to one part water sufficient to cover all the vegetables. Add 1 teaspoon salt for each 1 cup (250 ml) liquid used.

Pour a small amount of oil into a large skillet and fry each vegetable separately, including the garlic, hot peppers, and pears. As you finish frying each vegetable, add it to the others in a large bowl. While the vegetables are still warm, sprinkle the Bahar of Amba over them and stir. Place the vegetables into a large nonreactive bowl, and pour the liquid over. Transfer the mixture into washed and sterilized jars, and cover each jar with a sterilized lid. Store in a cool, shaded place, shaking or turning the jars upside down every few hours. After a day, taste the mixture and add salt if necessary. After 2 or 3 weeks, store in the refrigerator.

Basic Eggplant Salad

Eggplant, or aubergine, is generally considered the Israeli national vegetable, and every cook in Israel knows a hundred ways to prepare it. Page 40 offers a few variations of a most popular recipe. Amounts are approximate or have been omitted entirely; you can add or subtract whatever seems to be missing.

The most flavorful way to prepare the eggplant for the salad is to place it whole and unpeeled over a charcoal grill and allow it to blacken until soft inside. Failing that, you can place it over a gas flame on top of the stove, where it makes a bit of a mess as its liquid drips but it still emits a smoky flavor. Otherwise, it can be placed under a broiler (grill).

**About 2 lb (1 kg) large dark eggplants
(aubergines)**
$\frac{1}{4}$ cup (60 ml) olive or sunflower oil
**Lemon juice or white vinegar, according to
taste**

**Salt and freshly ground black pepper, to taste
Garlic, crushed then chopped (optional)**

Roast the eggplant as described above. When completely soft, blackened, and caved in, remove from heat. Do not rinse eggplant after it blackens.

Place eggplant on a cutting board and, using a sharp knife, slit it open and tilt the board over a sink to allow the liquid inside to run off. When the eggplant is cool enough to handle but still warm, use the knife to remove the peel and seeds.

The consistency of the salad depends on the method used for pulping the eggplant. Mashing it with a fork or pressing it through a potato masher results in a thick, pulpy mixture. Placing it in a food processor makes a smooth purée. I like to mash it with the spine of a knife. When the eggplant is mashed, place the pulp in a bowl and add the oil slowly while stirring, blending it in well. Add the lemon juice, freshly ground pepper, and salt to taste. This should all be done while the eggplant is still warm.

Lots of garlic can be added to make a dish that is called "caviar of the poor."

EGGPLANT SALADS

EGGPLANT WITH ONION AND TOMATO

1 portion Basic Eggplant Salad (see recipe, page 39)

2 tablespoons dried onion, or 3 tablespoons chopped fresh green (spring) onion
2 tomatoes, seeded and chopped
Parsley
Garnish: black olives

Mix eggplant with the remaining ingredients. Serve on a platter with black olives to dip.

Clockwise from top: Eggplant with Onion and Tomato, Eggplant with Peppers, and Eggplant with Feta.

EGGPLANT WITH FETA

1 portion Basic Eggplant Salad (see recipe, page 39)
1 cup (220 g) crumbled white feta cheese

Mix roasted eggplant with cheese and serve warm.

EGGPLANT WITH PEPPERS

1 portion Basic Eggplant Salad (see recipe, page 39)
4–5 red peppers, peeled, deseeded, and roasted; or 2–3 hot or sweet green peppers, peeled, deseeded, and chopped
Salt and pepper
1 tablespoon white vinegar

If using the red peppers, combine with the eggplant, salt, pepper, and vinegar in the bowl of a food processor and purée until smooth.

If using the green peppers, simply add them chopped to the basic eggplant salad recipe and serve.

EGGPLANT WITH PICKLE

1 portion Basic Eggplant Salad (see recipe, page 39)
$\frac{1}{2}$ cup (125 ml) mayonnaise
$\frac{1}{2}$ medium onion, chopped
1 dill pickle, chopped fine

Mix all ingredients and serve.

BABBAGHANOUJ

1 portion Basic Eggplant Salad (see recipe, page 39)
$\frac{1}{2}$ cup (125 ml) tahina paste
Garlic, crushed, to taste
Lemon juice to taste
Salt and freshly ground black pepper to taste

Garnish:
$\frac{1}{4}$ cup (60 ml) olive or sunflower oil
Pomegranate seeds

Mix the eggplant with the tahina paste. Add the crushed garlic and lemon juice as desired. Spread on a plate and serve topped with olive oil and pomegranate seeds.

HUMMUS

Everybody makes Hummus in Israel, and there is little doubt that the Arabs make the best. That is because they don't cut corners or make changes to the basic recipe, nor do they use modern food processors and other so-called improvements to prepare recipes that have been passed down to them through the ages. Hummus should be made by hand, using a mortar or grinder to mash the cooked chickpeas. Grinding them in a food processor or blender swells the chickpeas and gives them an unnatural consistency. Chickpeas for Hummus should be cooked until they are very soft. Adding baking soda will soften them faster, but it will affect the final flavor. They can, however, be cooked in a pressure cooker with no loss of flavor.

Hummus (top) and Musbacha (see recipe, page 128).

1 lb (500 g) raw chickpeas
2 medium onions, peeled
1–3 whole cloves garlic, peeled
Salt
$^1/_3$–$^1/_2$ cup (60–125 ml) tahina paste
1–3 cloves garlic, crushed
3–4 tablespoons lemon juice

Garnish:
2–3 cloves garlic, chopped fine
2 hot green peppers, chopped
$^1/_2$ cup parsley leaves, chopped
Olive oil
Zhoug (see recipe, page 36) (optional)

Place the chickpeas in a large bowl, cover with plenty of water, and allow to stand for 8 to 10 hours. If possible, change the water a number of times during the process.

Rinse the chickpeas. Place in a large pot with the onions and peeled garlic. Do not add salt. Cover with water and cook over a medium heat until very soft and falling apart (for at least 4 hours, unless using a pressure cooker). As the chickpeas cook, skim off the foam and additional skins that float to the surface of the water. When the chickpeas are cooked, remove the onions and garlic. Add salt and cook for another few minutes. Remove from the heat. Drain about three-quarters of the chickpeas, reserving some of the cooking liquid. Place the chickpeas in a bowl and mash with a mortar, masher, or grinder—but do not use a food processor! Mix in the tahina paste, crushed garlic, and 2 or 3 tablespoons of the lemon juice. Add some of the liquid in which the chickpeas were cooked, a little at a time, to arrive at a somewhat creamy consistency. Add more salt and lemon juice to taste.

Just prior to serving, spread some of the mixture onto individual small plates and top each with a few warm whole chickpeas. Add more chopped garlic, chopped green pepper, and a teaspoon of chopped parsley. Pour a generous amount of olive oil over all and serve with fresh pita. Add salt and Zhoug for those who like it even spicier. Serve with sliced onions, hot peppers, chopped tomatoes, or pickles.

FALAFEL

Falafel is actually an ancient dish introduced into Egypt by the Copts, descendants of the pharaohs, who today make up a community of nine million Egyptian Christians.

As a child born of Eastern European immigrants, I grew up convinced that Falafel was a purely Israeli invention, introduced by Yemenite Jews. Chickpeas, garlic, onions—put them together, spice them, fry them, and that's it. For the European Jewish immigrants who had been used to eating Gefilte Fish, this was a new and delightful taste. But Falafel was too spicy, and mouths were burned. Today, a Yemenite falafel vendor will always ask, "with zhoug, or without?".

The major difference between Egyptian and Israeli Falafel is the bean. In Egypt, Falafel is made with a flat white bean, called *ta'amiya*. Ancient seasonings are still used today. Falafel was introduced to Israel by the Arab population, who were the first people to substitute chickpeas for the white bean.

A nineteenth-century photograph shows an Arab Falafel vendor serving the dish in the same way as we eat it today, stuffed into a pita. Israeli enthusiasm over the chickpea Falafel has made it popular all over the Western world. Falafel vendors throughout Europe and America have given Israeli names to their stands, even though the vendors themselves may be Egyptian, Lebanese, or Jordanian.

1 lb (500 g) chickpeas
2 medium onions
5–8 cloves garlic, peeled
1 or 2 bunches parsley (leaves only) and/or cilantro (coriander) leaves
2–4 hot red peppers
1–2 teaspoons cumin
Salt and pepper to taste
1 tablespoon baking powder
1 tablespoon baking soda
Oil for frying

Rinse the chickpeas thoroughly, cover with water, and allow to stand overnight. The next day, drain the water and rinse the chickpeas again. Grind them with the onion, garlic, pepper, and the parsley and/or cilantro (coriander). If using an electric or manual grinder, put the ingredients through the grinder twice. A food processor also works well. Add the cumin, salt, freshly ground pepper, and baking powder. Transfer the mixture to a bowl and knead thoroughly.

Allow to rest for 30 minutes. Preheat oil in a deep frying pan. Just before frying, work in the baking soda, which helps the Falafel to expand. Roll the mixture into small balls or patties, using a specially-made Falafel scoop (an ice-cream scoop also works). Drop the balls into the hot oil and cook until they are golden. To serve, stuff the Falafel balls into warm pita and add any of the following: Tahina Sauce (page 35), sliced onion and parsley, cabbage or onion salad, hot and sour pickles, roasted eggplant, or a slice of roasted or fried potato.

ONION, PARSLEY & FRESH ZA'ATAR SALADS

ONION SALAD

Before preparing this salad, sprinkle the onion slices with coarse salt and allow them to stand for an hour. In this way they will lose their sharpness and acrid odor.

> 3 onions
> 1 teaspoon coarse salt
> 1 cup chopped mint leaves or chopped
>   parsley or celery leaves
> 1/2 cup (80 g) pomegranate seeds or 1 teaspoon
>   sumach (also known as rhus) (optional)
> Juice of 1/2 lemon
> 2–3 tablespoons olive oil

Clockwise from top: Fresh Za'atar Salad, Onion Salad and Parsley Salad.

Slice the onion thinly and place in a colander. Sprinkle the slices with coarse salt and allow them to drain for an hour. Squeeze the remaining water from the slices and transfer to a serving bowl. Add the mint leaves and the pomegranate seeds or sumac; then add the lemon juice and oil and serve.

PARSLEY SALAD

This parsley salad from the Diana Restaurant in Nazareth whets the appetite for the main course.

> 2 large bunches parsley, washed and stems
>   removed
> 2 hot green peppers, deseeded and shopped
> 1–2 firm ripe tomatoes, deseeded and cut into
>   1/4 in (1/2 cm) pieces
> 1 whole lemon, skinned, pithed, deseeded, and
>   diced
> Juice of 1 additional lemon

> 2 cloves garlic, crushed (optional)
> Salt to taste
> Olive oil

Chop the parsley and add the peppers, the tomatoes, and the lemon dice. Blend ingredients well. Add the lemon juice, garlic, salt, and oil and mix again.

FRESH ZA'ATAR SALAD

Za'atar is a wild hyssop plant that grows abundantly in the hills of Israel. It is recognizable by its strong scent when rubbed through the fingers, or when the wet grass begins to dry in the sun in the early morning. Oregano leaves can be used instead. Like oregano, za'atar leaves can be pulled off the stem against the direction of growth. This salad accompanies outdoor grilled meats. The stems of the za'atar can be thrown onto the grill to allow the aromas to permeate the fish or meat.

> 1 cup za'atar (or oregano) leaves
> 3–4 green (spring) onions
> Juice of 1 large lemon
> 2–3 tablespoons olive oil
> Salt to taste
> 1 hot green pepper (optional)

Place the za'atar leaves in a bowl. Clean the green (spring) onions and chop finely, including as much of the green as is edible. Add to the za'atar, along with the lemon juice, olive oil, and salt. Add the chopped pepper if you like it hot.

FATOUSH

Pita and Pomegranate Salad

This Arab salad uses the principles of the poor kitchen, incorporating as it does all the leftovers from other meals in addition to those ingredients on hand. Stale pita is broken into small pieces to absorb the flavors of the salad, making it a perfect snack or light meal.

3–4 firm ripe tomatoes
2–3 young cucumbers
1 medium onion or 3 green (spring) onions
1–2 hot peppers
$\frac{1}{2}$ cup chopped mint leaves
$\frac{1}{3}$ cup (90 ml) olive oil
Juice and finely chopped peel of 1 large lemon
1–2 stale or toasted pita breads
1 garlic clove, split
Seeds of 1 pomegranate (optional)
Salt to taste

Chop the tomatoes, cucumbers, onions, and peppers, transfer them all to a large bowl, and sprinkle with the mint leaves. Chop the lemon peel and add. Squeeze the lemon juice over the salad. Add the oil with a generous amount of salt and mix well.

Split the pita, rub the open end of the split garlic over it, tear into bite-sized pieces, and toss into the salad. Add the pomegranate seeds and mix well. Serve immediately.

AVOCADO SALAD WITH LABANEH AND MINT
& CUCUMBER SALAD WITH LABANEH

AVOCADO SALAD WITH LABANEH AND MINT

The farmers who first planted avocado trees on the coastal plain in the 1920s mashed the fruit into a pulp, added some chopped green (spring) onion, and flavored it with salt and lemon juice. Sometimes chopped hard-boiled eggs or mayonnaise were added to the pulp. The avocado soon became a winter delicacy.

The usual way of serving avocado in Israel is mashed, salted, and spread on a slice of bread. In addition to lemon juice, one can add crushed garlic, horseradish, paprika or chile pepper, Zhoug (page 36), soft white goat cheese, yogurt, sour cream, smoked salmon, or Labaneh (page 37), as in the following recipe.

Avacado Salad with Labaneh and Mint (top), and Cucumber Salad with Labaneh.

2 ripe avocados
4 sprigs mint (leaves only), chopped
1 clove garlic, crushed
4 tablespoons Labaneh (see recipe, page 37), or sour cream
Olive oil
Juice of ½ lemon
Salt to taste

Slice the avocado in half, remove the pit, and scrape out the pulp. Mash with a fork, or dice, and place in a bowl. Add the chopped mint leaves, crushed garlic, Labaneh, olive oil, and lemon juice. Taste and add salt if necessary.

CUCUMBER SALAD WITH LABANEH

½ teaspoon salt
2 tablespoons mint leaves, crushed; or chopped dill
4–5 small firm cucumbers
1 cup (250 ml) Labaneh (see recipe, page 37)
3 tablespoons olive oil

Mix the mint or dill together with the salt in a large bowl. Rinse the cucumbers, then chop (peeled or unpeeled) into small cubes, and add to the bowl with the herbs. Mix well. Spread the Labaneh on a serving dish, add the chopped cucumbers, sprinkle with the olive oil, and serve.

CHOPPED LIVER & POTATO SALAD

CHOPPED LIVER

A characteristic of European Jewish cooking is to combine inexpensive ingredients with something more costly, thereby enriching the diet while extending the servings. As chickens produce only a single liver, hard-boiled eggs and fried onions were added to make that single liver feed more people.

1 lb (500 g) chicken livers, rinsed
Freshly ground pepper
3–4 medium onions, peeled and sliced thinly
1/4 cup (60 ml) vegetable oil or 3 tablespoons goose (or chicken) fat
3–4 hard-boiled eggs
Salt to taste
1 additional onion, peeled and sliced thinly (optional)

Potato Salad (top) and Chopped Liver served with bread.

To kasher (or conform to Jewish dietary laws) the livers, burn them gently over an open fire and sprinkle with salt to remove any remaining blood. Add some freshly ground pepper. Fry the sliced onions in the oil or fat until golden brown. Remove with a slotted spoon and set aside.

Reheat the oil or chicken fat, add the livers, and fry just until they lose their pink color. Remove from the heat. Return the onions to the pan, add salt, and allow to cool. Grate or grind the livers with the onions and eggs. Do not use a food processor. Taste and add salt if necessary.

If desired, fry the additional onion until golden and sprinkle some water on top to fry until crisp (be careful of the spatter!). Serve the chopped liver with the crisp fried onion on top.

POTATO SALAD

Potato salad came to Israel by way of immigrant Jews from Germany, who prepared it in their own special way: cooked cubed potatoes adorned with pickles, apples, and chopped onion, and dressed with mayonnaise and vinegar. Christian Arabs in Israel prefer a different kind of potato salad, made with more local ingredients: olive oil, lemon juice, and spicy green peppers. The olive oil must be fresh and of good quality.

4 potatoes, cooked and peeled
1–2 spicy green peppers
1 clove garlic, crushed
Juice of 1 large lemon
1/3 cup (90 ml) high-quality olive oil
Salt to taste
1/2 cup chopped parsley or mint leaves (optional)
2 green (spring) onions, chopped (optional)

Dice the potatoes or slice them fairly thinly. Remove the stem and seeds of the pepper, and chop. Mix in all the other ingredients. If using parsley and green (spring) onions, add more olive oil and lemon juice.

SHAKSHOUKA

Fried Peppers and Tomatoes with Eggs

To learn how to make the perfect shakshouka, I went to Jaffa to visit Bino, who is known there as the "shakshouka doctor." This delicious egg and vegetable dish is easy to make—once you know how it's done.

4 tablespoons vegetable oil
2–3 hot green peppers
3–4 cloves garlic, peeled and coarsely chopped
4–5 small tomatoes, coarsely chopped
Salt to taste
1–2 tablespoons hot or sweet paprika,
    or half of each, according to taste
4 eggs

Heat the oil in a frying pan over medium heat. Chop the pepper coarsely into it, then add the chopped garlic and tomato. Turn up the heat and sauté until the tomatoes are soft. Scrape the mixture from the sides of the pan into the oil. Sprinkle over some salt, allow the liquids to evaporate somewhat, and mix well. After about 8 minutes, add the paprika and mix again. Continue to sauté for a further 2 minutes.

Break the eggs one at a time into a small dish. Gently slide each egg into the pan over the tomatoes. With a spoon, carefully fold the whites into the tomatoes without breaking the yolks. When the whites have set but the yolks are still soft, remove from the heat and serve. Challah is the best accompaniment, but a baguette is also fine.

GOLDENE YOICH

Chicken Soup with Matzo Meal Dumplings

Chicken soup in Israel is the typical chicken soup of Eastern European Jews. Its most important characteristic is its aroma. Every Friday morning, often even on Thursday afternoons, homes and streets are filled with the aroma of chicken soup being prepared for the Friday evening Sabbath meal.

I have occasionally found myself entering the hallway of an apartment block and pausing to take in the aromas in an attempt to discover behind which door a Jewish grandmother is preparing soup, in the hope of persuading her to impart her secrets. However, it was not until Grandmother Sonya Kaplan kindly parted with her chicken soup recipe that I met with any success. I began preparing the soup with some skepticism, but as it came to a boil, I recognized its aroma at once.

There are two tricks to the method: the first is to cover the bottom of the pot with bunches of parsley and dill, along with their stems. The contact with the direct heat imparts a special flavor and reduces the amount of bubbling. The second trick is to just cover the chicken with water, using as little liquid as possible.

Chicken Soup with Matzo Meal Dumplings, or Knaidlach (see recipe for Knaidlach, page 128).

1 bunch parsley
2 bunches dill
1 whole chicken (about 3 lb or 1.5 kg)
1–2 celery roots, cut into chunks
2 onions, quartered
3–4 carrots, each cut in half
1 potato, quartered
5 whole black peppercorns
Coarse salt
Pinch of sugar
$1/_2$ green pepper (optional)
1–2 cloves garlic, peeled (optional)
1–2 allspice kernels (optional)
Feet and gizzard of the chicken (optional)

Place the parsley and dill stalks on the bottom of a large soup pot. Rinse the chicken in cold water and place it on top. Peel the celery roots, onions, carrots, and potato and tuck them in and around the chicken. Add the whole peppercorns, salt to taste, sugar, and any or all of the optional ingredients. Add only 6 cups (1.5 litres) water. Bring the pot to a boil and simmer gently for 1 to $1\frac{1}{2}$ hours. Remove the chicken, and separate the meat from the carcass. Put some of the meat back into the stock, and reserve the rest of the meat for a second course. Taste and correct the seasoning.

Cool the soup, and if desired, place in the refrigerator overnight to allow the fat to collect at the top of the pot. Skim, reheat and add the customary Matzo Meal Dumplings or Knaidlach (see recipe, page 128), noodles, *kreplach* (stuffed ravioli), or croutons.

HEARTY LENTIL SOUP

Lentil soup is a popular dish in Israel, and it has many variations. The recipe always begins with fried onions, but other additions differ from community to community. Israelis of Moroccan descent consider chopped cilantro (coriander) leaves essential. Eastern Europeans often add sausage or smoked meat to their lentil soup. Some Israelis add a little lemon to make it perfect. Others add thin egg noodles, or beet stems to make it green.

Orange lentils dissolve during cooking. Brown and green lentils maintain their shape, and can be ground as well. As a rule, the fresher the lentil, the better flavor it has and the less swelling it causes in the stomach. Add salt only at the end of cooking; salt tends to prevent beans and lentils from softening.

In Genesis (25:29–32), Esau sold his biblical birthright in exchange for lentil soup. Which recipe was it? Here is one Israeli version.

- 1 lb (500 g) brown or orange lentils
- 1 large or 2 medium onions
- 2 cloves garlic, peeled and chopped
- 2–4 beef marrow bones (optional)
- 2 stalks celery, chopped
- Ground black pepper
- Salt or beef bouillon (stock cube)
- ½ teaspoon paprika, turmeric, and/or cumin (optional)

Garnish:
- 1 bunch cilantro (coriander), parsley, or celery leaves, chopped
- Fresh lemon wedges
- Toast or sliced baguette

Pick the lentils over carefully; there is always a danger of small, tooth-breaking stones. Cover them with water and soak for 3 or 4 hours. Drain.

In the bottom of a large soup pot, sauté the onions until soft and then add the garlic. Continue to sauté for another minute and then add the lentils, bone marrow, celery, and 6 or 7 cups (1.5 to 1.75 litres) water. Bring to a boil, lower the heat, and simmer for about 1½ hours until the lentils are soft. Add salt or a bouillon cube and add some ground black pepper to taste. Add paprika, turmeric, or cumin, as desired. Cook for a few minutes longer, taste for seasoning, and add more salt if necessary. The soup can also be blended before seasoning to make a velvety purée.

To serve, ladle the soup into bowls. Sprinkle the chopped cilantro (coriander), parsley, or celery leaves on top and place a lemon wedge on the edge of the soup plate. Accompany with a slice of toast on which to spread the bone marrow. If bone marrow is not used, the toast can be rubbed with half a clove of garlic and drizzled with olive oil. Alternatively, the toast may be placed on the bottom of each bowl and the soup poured over it.

KIBBEH SOUP

Beet and Turnip Soup with Beef Dumplings

Every Friday at lunchtime, the Kurdish or Iraqi Jews of Jerusalem disappear from the streets, sneaking off to their mothers and grandmothers to have a dish of what is known as their "love potion", Kibbeh soup.

For the stuffing:
2 chopped onions
3 tablespoons vegetable oil
1 lb (500 g) ground beef
Salt or powdered bouillon (stock cube) to taste
Freshly ground black pepper
Pinch of ground allspice

For the dough:
1 slice day-old bread
2 ³/₄ cups (500 g) semolina (or cream of wheat)
2 tablespoons flour
2 tablespoons vegetable oil
2 tablespoons margarine, softened
Salt or powdered bouillon (stock cube) to taste

For the soup:
1 large onion
1 tablespoon vegetable oil
10 cups (2.5 litres) clear chicken soup or bouillon (stock)
1 beet, peeled and sliced
1 turnip, peeled and sliced
4–5 stalks celery, chopped
Leaves of 4–5 parsley stalks, chopped
Leaves of 4–5 cilantro (coriander) stalks, chopped
Leaves of 4–5 beets, chopped
2–3 tablespoons tomato paste
5–6 cloves garlic, sliced
1 teaspoon sugar
1 teaspoon lemon salt, or juice of 1 large lemon
Vegetable oil for frying

To make the **stuffing**, fry the chopped onions in oil until soft. Add the meat and crumble it as it fries. As the meat loses its raw color, add 1½ cups (375 ml) boiling water. Cover the pot partially and continue cooking until liquid evaporates and the meat is thoroughly cooked. Add seasoning and mix well.

To make the **dough**, wet the bread and squeeze out the water. Mix the semolina and flour and add the bread. Mix well. Add the other ingredients and mix again. Add ⅓ cup (90 ml) water and blend until the mixture is a smooth and pliable dough. To assemble the dumplings, form plum-sized balls and cover all with a wet cloth. With moistened hands, make a dent in each ball, stuff it with about 1 tablespoon of the filling, and close the dough around the filling. Set aside.

To make the **soup**, fry the onions in oil over medium heat. Add the chicken stock, beet, turnip, celery, herbs, and beet leaves. When the vegetables are soft, add the tomato paste and garlic. Dissolve the sugar and lemon salt (or lemon juice) in ½ cup (125 ml) boiling water and add to the soup. Taste and season if necessary. As the soup boils, add the dumplings and continue to cook for 45 minutes.

CHICKPEA SOUP WITH SQUID AND PARMESAN

Haim Cohen, Keren Restaurant, Jaffa

The Keren Restaurant is housed in a historic small wooden building brought all the way from Maine, USA, by 157 American colonists in 1866. It opened in the 1980s as a French restaurant, and chef Cohen's philosophy has always been that dishes should come from natural sources. The restaurant has slowly evolved to connect to its surroundings. "One has to find ingredients commonly used," says Cohen. "I try to use flavors we like and are accustomed to, and bring them to the environs of Jaffa."

About 2$\frac{1}{2}$ cups (600 g) raw chickpeas, soaked overnight
About 5 cups (1.25 litres) chicken stock
$\frac{1}{2}$ lb (250 g) Parmesan cheese, grated
Salt to taste
1 whole pita
4 whole squid, heads intact
Olive oil
2 stalks fresh za'atar or oregano

Drain the chickpeas from their water and place in a large soup pot. Cover with fresh water and cook over medium heat until completely soft. Drain and measure 4 cups chickpeas; blend them in a food processor, then press through a sieve. Reserve the remaining chickpeas in their water for garnishing the dish. Place the purée back into the pot, pour in the chicken stock, and add the cheese. Bring to a gentle boil over a low heat. Taste, adding salt if needed. If the soup is too thick, it can be diluted with the water in which the chickpeas were cooked.

Cut the pita into bite-sized pieces. Clean the squid and slice the body into round strips. Heat 3 tablespoons of olive oil in a frying pan and fry the squid, including the heads, until they become translucent, about 2 minutes.

Put a few whole cooked chickpeas and some pieces of pita into each of four soup bowls, along with 3 to 4 fresh za'atar or oregano leaves. Pour over the soup, place the squid in the center, and serve immediately.

PITA & KA'AK

PITA

Most Israelis buy their pita at the local bakery or in a grocery or supermarket. However, it is an easy bread to prepare at home if the oven can be heated to a really high temperature. Be sure to fully preheat the oven before the dough goes in, for it is the abrupt change in temperature that causes the bread to puff and make its famous pocket!

1 tablespoon dry yeast, or 1 sachet
1 teaspoon sugar or honey
5 $^{3}/_{4}$ cups (1 kg) flour
1 tablespoon salt

Dissolve the yeast with the sugar or honey in $^{1}/_{4}$ cup (60 ml) lukewarm water and allow to stand for 10 minutes until it bubbles. In a large bowl, mix the flour with the salt and add the yeast mixture and 3 cups (750 ml) water. Mix well and knead until the dough becomes smooth and pliable but is still a bit sticky. Place the dough in a bowl and cover with plastic wrap or a kitchen towel. Allow to stand in a warm place for an hour, or until doubled.

Preheat the oven to 425–450°F (220–230°C, gas mark 7–8). Divide the dough into 12 pieces and form each into a small ball. Spread some flour on the counter or tabletop. Press each ball of dough into a round about $^{1}/_{4}$ in ($^{1}/_{2}$ cm) thick. Flour a cookie sheet (baking tray) and place each pita on it. (Do not worry if the balls are a bit sticky and not perfectly round.) Bake for 8 to 10 minutes. Once out of the oven, place the pitas in a paper bag, or wrap in a dry, clean kitchen towel.

Helpful hints: Assorted breads may be made using the basic pita dough. Flatten dough balls to $^{1}/_{4}$ in ($^{1}/_{2}$ cm) thick and make indents in the surface with your finger. For Pita with Za'atar, top the dough with za'atar and olive oil and bake as for Pita. Alternatively, top the dough with egg, or a mixture of meat and onions before baking. For Sambusak, fill the dough with salted white cheese and fold.

KA'AK

This crisp and savory, sesame-covered, bagel-shaped bread uses a moister version of pita dough.

1 tablespoon dry yeast, or 1 sachet
1 teaspoon sugar or honey
5 $^{3}/_{4}$ cups (1 kg) flour
1 tablespoon salt
Handful sesame seeds

Mix and knead as for pita, but add 3$^{1}/_{4}$ cups (800 ml) water to the flour and yeast mixture. Prepare balls as large as apples and let them rise for 30 minutes. Make a hole in the middle of each ball and stretch the dough out into a ring. Dip first in milk and then in a pile of sesame seeds. Place on a greased pan, and bake at 375°F (190°C, gas mark 5) for about 20 minutes, then lower the temperature to 225°F (110°C, gas mark $^{1}/_{3}$) and bake for 15 minutes.

JERUSALEM KUGEL

Savory Noodle and Egg Pastry

Jerusalem Kugel is a brown noodle and egg pastry, spiced with black pepper and sweetened with brown sugar. It is baked in the oven the entire night on a low setting to be served the following day, usually on the Sabbath.

One of my favorite childhood memories is the Jerusalem Kugel served after synagogue on Sabbath mornings. Near the end of the service, the kugels were wheeled in on a cart from the bakery, covered with sheets and layers of wool to keep them warm. I would push between the congregants to watch as the kugels were put onto trays and cut into slices with a string. The kugel was oily and sweet, but also spicy. In one hand I held the kugel, in the other a sour dill pickle. I alternated bites, feeling the spiciness of one and the sourness of the other, enjoying them both enormously. In the stillness of the moment, all one could hear were the sounds of people munching.

1 lb (500 g) thin flat egg noodles
1 cup (250 ml) vegetable oil
1 cup (200 g) sugar
1 tablespoon freshly ground black pepper
Salt to taste
6 eggs, beaten

Preheat the oven to 300˚F (150˚C, gas mark 2). Cook the noodles in boiling salted water until they soften just to the bite. Drain and place in a large bowl. Heat the oil and sugar in a saucepan over a low heat, shaking the pan until the sugar melts and turns brown, about 10 minutes. Stir the mixture into the noodles.

Beat the eggs and add to the noodles together with the salt and pepper, stirring until the seasonings are well distributed. Grease an ovenproof casserole and pour the noodle mixture into it. Flatten with a spoon and cover with lightly greased parchment paper before sealing the pot with a lid.

Bake for 30 minutes in the preheated oven and then reduce the heat to 200˚F (100˚C, gas mark ¼) and bake for 7 to 10 hours. If the kugel begins to dry and burn, add a little water. However, if it has been properly covered with aluminum foil, this should not happen. Serve with brined cucumbers.

PATIRA

Herb-stuffed Pastry Triangles

Patira, an Arab specialty, are fried pastries filled with a herbed stuffing of young leaves of "Egyptian clove," a plant that grows underneath olive trees and, in spring, covers the ground with a pink and lavender carpet. Spinach leaves, beet greens, or a mixture of za'atar and green (spring) onions can be substituted. The pastries are eaten together with cracked green olives and a small chopped vegetable salad.

For the dough:
> 2 ³/₄ cups (500 g) flour
> 1 tablespoon yeast, or 1 sachet
> Salt to taste

Patira (right), and Eggplant and Cheese Pies, or Borekas, served with eggs (see recipe, page 130).

For the herb filling:
> ³/₄ lb (375 g) chopped fresh za'atar or oregano leaves, stems removed
> ³/₄ lb (375 g)chopped green onions
> Salt to taste
> ¹/₄ cup (60 ml) olive oil
> Lemon juice

For the spinach or Swiss chard filling:
> 1¹/₂-2 lb (750 g–1 kg) spinach or Swiss chard
> ¹/₄ cup (60 ml) olive oil
> 2 onions, finely chopped
> 1 to 2 tablespoons sumach (rhus)
> Pinch cumin
> Salt

> Oil for deep frying (the pastries can be baked if preferred.)

To make the **dough**, mix all ingredients and add enough lukewarm water to form a soft, smooth, and even slightly sticky dough. Knead briefly, cover with a damp cloth, and allow to rise for 1 hour.

To make the **herb filling**, wash the herb leaves thoroughly, squeeze out the water, and mix well with the other ingredients.

To make the **spinach or Swiss chard filling**, remove the ribs, then rinse the leaves and cook in a covered pot without water for a few minutes. Squeeze out the liquids and chop. Fry the onions in the oil until brown. Mix in the sumach, cumin, and salt to taste. Add the onion mixture to the spinach or chard.

To assemble, tear off pieces of dough about the size of an egg and roll each into a ball. Cover with a towel, and let rest for several minutes. Flour a work surface, and with oiled hands flatten each ball into a round. Place a teaspoon of filling on top of each round and fold into a triangle, using a fork to poke holes in each ball. Deep-fry the pastries in oil, or bake in a medium oven, until golden.

MEAT-FILLED BAKED PASTRIES (PASTELICOS)

Simcha Sofer, Barud, Jerusalem

In Ladino, the Spanish-Jewish dialect, *pastel* means "stuffed dough." Pastelicos are small stuffed patties, the pride of Sephardic Jewish cooks. Many varieties exist, ranging from the Borekas (see photograph, page 69) of Turkey and the Balkans to the *pastels* of Salonika (a notable Jewish community in Greece until World War II). It is customary to serve the Pastelicos with hard-boiled eggs and Spicy Chopped Salad (see recipe, page 130).

Meat-filled Baked Pastries (Pastelicos), served with Spicy Chopped Salad (see recipe, page 130) and hard-boiled eggs.

For the dough:

7 tablespoons (100 g) salted margarine (butter)
$1/2$ cup (125 ml) sunflower or corn oil
$1/2$ teaspoon salt
2 $3/4$ cups (500 g) flour
1 teaspoon baking powder

For the filling:

3–4 tablespoons sunflower oil
1 large onion, chopped
1 lb (500 g) ground beef
Salt and freshly ground pepper
3 to tablespoons pine nuts

To coat:

1 egg yolk, beaten
Handful sesame seeds

To make the **dough**, boil 1 cup (250 ml) water in a saucepan together with the margarine or butter, vegetable oil, and salt until the margarine or butter is melted into the water. Remove from the heat.

Place the flour and baking powder in a large bowl and combine with the liquid. Mix well, cover, and allow to cool. When the mixture is cool enough to handle, knead it until it forms a soft, pliable, and smooth dough. Wrap the dough in plastic wrap and place in a cool corner of the kitchen for at least 30 minutes, but do not refrigerate.

To make the **filling**, sauté the onion in the oil until translucent. Add the ground beef, a pinch of salt, and a good grinding of black pepper. Stir, crumbling the meat with a fork. When the meat loses its pink color, add 4 tablespoons of water and cook for 5 to 10 minutes. Mix in the pine nuts.

To assemble, heat the oven to 350°F (180°C, gas mark 4). Flatten the dough with a rolling pin until it is $1/8$-in ($1/2$-cm) thick. Cut out circles using the rim of a large glass. Shape the circles, one by one, into little pots. Use small balls of the leftover dough to fashion lids for each "pot." Fill the cups with the beef filling and top each with a lid. Pinch the edges together to seal them. Place the pastries on an oiled baking sheet, brush with the egg yolk diluted with 1 teaspoon of water, and sprinkle with sesame seeds. Bake until golden.

LACHMA BA'AJEEN

Meat-topped Pastries

I have eaten Lachma Ba'ajeen at a restaurant in the Armenian quarter of the Old City of Jerusalem, and again at the home of a Lebanese Jewish family in the coastal town of Bat Yam, just south of Tel Aviv. The second time, it was even better than I had remembered it. This is an anonymous offering from the woman who prepared it for me.

For the dough:

1 tablespoon dry yeast, or 1 sachet
$^1/_4$ teaspoon sugar
2 $^3/_4$ cups (500 g) flour
$^1/_2$ teaspoon salt
3 tablespoons vegetable oil

For the filling:

3 tablespoons olive oil
3–4 onions, finely chopped
1–2 tomatoes, skinned, deseeded, and finely chopped
2 lb (1 kg) ground meat (preferably lamb)
1 tablespoon pomegranate sauce (optional)
1–1 $^1/_2$ cups (125 to 180 g) pine nuts
Salt and freshly ground black pepper to taste

To make the **dough**, dissolve the yeast and sugar in 1 cup (250 ml) lukewarm water. Allow to stand for 10 minutes while the yeast froths. Meanwhile, mix the flour with the salt and oil in a large bowl. Add the yeast mixture and enough lukewarm water to make a soft, smooth, slightly sticky, but pliable dough. Knead briefly, cover with plastic wrap or a towel, and place the bowl near a warm place for 30 minutes until it expands.

To make the **filling**, in a large frying pan, sauté the onions in 3 tablespoons olive oil until they are translucent. Add the tomatoes, and continue to sauté until all the liquid has evaporated. Remove the pan and add the meat, pomegranate sauce, pine nuts, salt, and pepper. Mix together well.

To assemble, use oiled hands to form the dough into small, walnut-sized balls. Flatten each ball and place on a greased baking sheet. Sprinkle each round with some meat filling and press it into a closed package. Alternatively, the round of dough can be rolled into a cylinder and then curled up into a snail shape.

Heat the oven to 425˚F (220˚C, gas mark 7). Place the pastries on a baking tray in the oven and bake until the sides turn golden, about 8 to 10 minutes. Remove from oven, and while the pastries are still hot, place them one on top of another to keep the dough from drying out. Serve with lemon wedges.

MALAUACH & JACHNUN

Yemenite Breads

MALAUACH

2³/₄ cups (500 g) flour
1¹/₂ cups (375 ml) water
1 tablespoon plain white or citrus vinegar
1 teaspoon salt
7 tablespoons (100 g) good-quality margarine

Mix together all the ingredients except the margarine and knead to a smooth dough. Cover with a towel and knead again after 30 minutes. Cover again and knead a third time after another 30 minutes. Repeat a fourth time. Divide the dough into 6 equal parts, form each into a round ball, cover again, and allow to rest for yet another 30 minutes. The dough has taken more than 2 hours to reach this stage.

Grease a work surface with a litle oil, then melt the margarine. Working with one ball of dough at a time, spread it out over the greased work surface, roll it, and stretch it into the thinnest possible layer. It does not matter if it tears somewhat. Brush the pastry layer with the melted margarine and fold one side one-third of the way over. Brush again with melted margarine. Fold the opposite side down over the first to form a rectangle, and roll the dough into the shape of a tube. Place in the refrigerator for 3 hours. Now roll each tube of dough into a thin layer and fry in oil on both sides. Serve with Zhoug (see recipe, page 36).

JACHNUN

5³/₄ cups (1 kg) flour
2 tablespoons sugar
1 teaspoon baking powder
1 tablespoon salt
14 tablespoons (about 1³/₄ sticks, 220 g) margarine
2 heaped tablespoons honey

Mix the flour with the sugar, baking powder, and salt. Slowly add about 2¹/₂ cups (625 ml) lukewarm water until the mixture forms a sticky dough. Knead well until the dough no longer sticks to the hands. Cover with a towel and allow to stand in a warm place for 20 minutes. Meantime, melt the margarine over a low heat and add the honey. Divide the rested dough into 12 equal portions and form each into a ball. Cover and allow to stand for another 15 to 20 minutes.

Pour some of the margarine mixture onto a large work surface and spread. Prepare tubes as in the previous recipe for Malauach, and arrange the tubes in 2 rows on a greased baking dish. Bake in a very hot oven, uncovered, for 30 minutes then add ¹/₃ cup (90 ml) water, cover and bake overnight in the lowest possible oven, about 200°F (100°C, gas mark ¹/₂). Serve with Zhoug (see recipe, page 36). Eggs are traditionally eaten with the Jachnun bread on the following day.

*Malauach (left)
with hard-boiled
eggs, and
Jachnun.*

STUFFED VINE LEAVES

Young round vine (grape) leaves are traditionally used for wrapping. They have the best flavor—gently tangy—and are easy to work with. The custom of stuffing grape leaves with rice was invented by the Turks, who brought the recipe with them when they invaded the Holy Land in the sixteenth century. Although most of the stuffings are a combination of meat and rice, different fillings have evolved among the various communities. Local Armenians stuff them with lentils; the Greeks like them with meat seasoned like kebabs. Others stuff them with white goat cheese or a whole fat cheese. If fresh vine leaves are not available, brined leaves can be purchased in specialty shops but they should be rinsed in warm water before use.

Stuffed Vine Leaves served with Yogurt Sauce for Stuffed Vine Leaves (see recipe, page 37).

About 80 young vine leaves
2 onions, chopped
5–6 tablespoons olive, corn, or sunflower oil, divided
³/₄ cup (100 g) pine nuts or roasted sunflower seeds
1¹/₂ cups washed long-grain rice
About ¹/₂ lb (250 g) ground or chopped fresh lamb (optional)
1 tomato, chopped, with juice and seeds removed (optional)
3 tablespoons chopped mint leaves
1 teaspoon salt
Pinch of freshly ground pepper
Pinch of paprika
Juice of 1 lemon, divided

If using brined vine leaves, soak them for 30 minutes and rinse thoroughly. If using fresh leaves, scald for a few seconds in boiling water. Trim the stems from the leaves and arrange some of the leaves on the base of a large, wide-bottomed pot big enough to hold all the rolled leaves.

Sauté the onions in about 3 tablespoons of the oil until they are translucent. Add the pine nuts and fry for another few minutes. Add the rice and, if desired, the lamb, and tomato. Mix well and remove from the heat. Add the mint leaves, salt, black pepper, paprika, and half the lemon juice. Stir well.

To stuff each leaf, lay the leaf flat, shiny side down. Place a teaspoon of the filling close to the stem end, fold the sides in, and roll tightly from the stem side upwards.

Arrange the stuffed leaves so that they fit tightly over the flat leaves, if possible in just two layers. Cover with one more layer of fresh whole vine leaves. Boil 1¹/₂ cups (375 ml) water with the remaining lemon juice and oil, and some paprika. Pour the liquid over the vine leaves to cover. Place a dinner plate on top of the stuffed leaves, cover the pot, and cook over medium heat. Allow to simmer gently for 20 to 25 minutes. Leave the pot covered for another 30 minutes before serving. Serve with Yogurt Sauce for Stuffed Vine Leaves (see recipe, page 37).

STUFFED FIGS WITH GOOSE LIVER

Moise Peer, Mishkenot Shaananim, Jerusalem

This combination of juicy figs with the goose liver and its accompanying sweet sauce is a sensual delight, as well as a brilliant way of combining ancient and modern foods of Israel.

20 dried figs
½ lb (250 g) goose liver, cut into small pieces
Salt and white pepper to taste
Handful fresh tarragon leaves, chopped
2 cups (500 ml) clear stock
⅔ cup (150 ml) Benedictine liqueur

Preheat the oven to 350°F (180°C, gas mark 4). With a sharp knife, make a slit at the stem-end of each fig, prizing it open with a finger. Sprinkle the chopped livers with salt, white pepper, and the chopped tarragon leaves. Stuff each fig carefully with a small amount of this mixture. Place the stuffed figs, stem (stuffed) side up, in one layer in an ovenproof dish. Pour the stock and liqueur over them and cover with aluminum foil. Place in the preheated oven and bake for about 25 minutes, until the sauce has reduced and thickened.

STUFFED ARTICHOKES WITH AGRISTADA SAUCE

Agristada, a warm, thick, mayonnaise-like sauce made of eggs and lemon juice, is popular among Greek, Turkish, and Bulgarian Jews. It is a simple sauce, suffused with legend and popular myths.

Some say agristada must be made only by whisking, while others claim that simply whipping it with a fork is just as good. It should be made in an enamel pot so that it doesn't take on any of the flavor of a metal pan.

When I first prepared agristada successfully, I felt, "Yasu! Now I am one of you!" and decided that this sauce would be an integral part of my cuisine. Rich, velvety, and yellow, it is like a covering robe. Its delicate, tangy flavor goes well with fried brains and fish, chicken livers, sliced cooked chicken, and meat or vegetable cutlets.

6 fresh artichokes, tough leaves and choke removed

Salt
$\frac{1}{4}$ cup (60 ml) oil
1 tablespoon flour plus additional flour for coating
1 calf's brain
2 tablespoons vinegar

For the agristada sauce:

1 tablespoon flour
2 eggs, beaten
Juice of $1\frac{1}{2}$ large lemons
Salt to taste

Put the artichoke hearts in a pot with enough water to cover them. Add a little salt, 1 teaspoon of oil, and 1 tablespoon of flour. Cook the artichokes until they are soft, about 20 minutes. Drain, reserving the liquid.

Soak the brain in cold water made sour with 2 tablespoons of vinegar. Remove the capillaries and the membrane coating. Cut the brain into thick slices. Dry each slice of brain, dip in flour, and shake off the excess. Heat about 2 tablespoons of oil in a frying pan, fry each slice on both sides, add $\frac{1}{4}$ cup (60 ml) water, cover, and simmer for 15 minutes. Remove the brain, leaving the liquid in the pan, and set aside.

In a bowl, slowly dilute the flour in $1\frac{1}{4}$ cups (300 ml) of the artichoke water and stir until there are no lumps. Add the eggs and lemon juice and pour this mixture into the pan in which the brains were cooked. Cook gently over a low heat, whisking continuously, until the sauce thickens and reaches the point just before it bubbles—it is very important not to let it bubble and curdle. Remove from the heat. To serve, arrange the artichoke hearts on a plate and stuff each with a slice of brain. Pour over the sauce. Serve lukewarm or at room temperature.

KIBBEH NAAYA

Cracked Wheat and Lamb Cakes

Kibbeh Naaya is considered a delicacy by Syrians, Lebanese, and Druze Israelis, and it is found in the local Armenian cuisine as well. It comes from Zahalla, a region in Lebanon famous also for its arak, the anise-flavored drink popular throughout the Middle East. Arak is drunk with *meze*, or small simple peasant dishes, the most special being Kibbeh Naaya.

Note that traditionally the lamb in this dish is eaten raw so only the finest quality freshly slaughtered lamb is used. For a similar dish of cooked lamb and cracked wheat, see the recipe for Kibbeh Mahshiyeh on page 84.

1$^1\!/_2$ lb (750 g) ground bulgur (cracked wheat)
1 lb (500 g) extra lean, twice-ground lamb
1 teaspoon freshly ground black pepper
$^1\!/_2$ teaspoon ground allspice
1 heaped teaspoon salt

Optional additions:

Pinch of cinnamon
5–6 small basil leaves, chopped fine
1 small onion, grated
1 small tomato, chopped
Chopped parsley
Cumin, cayenne pepper, and 1 tablespoon
   tomato paste
$^1\!/_4$ cup (30 g) pine nuts

In a large bowl, cover the cracked wheat with water and mix by hand to remove the dirt and extra starch. Rinse and soak again in clean water for 30 minutes. Strain the water and dry thoroughly, squeezing the wheat to remove as much moisture as possible.

Mix the wheat with the meat, adding the pepper, allspice, and salt. Blend in additional optional ingredients if desired. Knead the mixture well until all the ingredients are completely blended. The mixture should be soft; if it seems dry, add a few teaspoons of water.

To serve, work the mixture into finger-like patties and serve with lemon juice or with a sauce made from olive oil, lemon juice, paprika, whole roasted peanuts and a little chopped green (spring) onion. The mixture may also be scooped up using lettuce leaves, if desired.

KIBBEH MAHSHIYEH

Fried Stuffed Kibbeh

Syrian and Lebanese women are proud of their touch, the special "finger" or "hand" that it takes to make a delicate kibbeh. The saying goes that a woman is blessed to be born with the long finger that eases the kibbeh making—a slight exaggeration, in my opinion. The shaping of the long slim kibbeh with its sharp ends is certainly an acquired skill, but anyone eager to succeed can learn it with ease. When stuffing, take care not to let the filling touch the edges of the dough—the oil from the meat will prevent a proper seal.

Fried, Stuffed Kibbeh (below), and Cracked Wheat Salad, or Tabouleh (see recipe, page 129).

For the dough:

Kibbeh Naaya (see recipe, page 82)
3 tablespoons flour

For the stuffing:

3–4 tablespoons vegetable oil
¹/₂ cup (60 g) pine nuts
1 lb (500 g) ground beef or lamb
2 large onions, finely chopped
1 teaspoon salt
¹/₂ teaspoon ground pepper
Pinch ground allspice
Pinch cinnamon
Oil for deep frying

To make the **dough**, add the flour to the Kibbeh Naaya recipe and knead to make a soft mixture, adding a little water if necessary.

To make the **stuffing**, fry the pine nuts in the oil until they are translucent. Set aside. In the same oil, fry the meat until it is very well done, separating with a fork. Add the chopped onion and spices and continue to sauté until the onion is well cooked. Remove from the heat and add the pine nuts. Set aside.

To assemble the kibbeh, take a lump of the dough with wetted hands and round it to about the size of an apricot. Make a deep hole with your finger, Fill the hole with 2 teaspoons of the filling and press the dough back together to cover the stuffing. Roll into a long oval shape, making a point at each end. Fry in deep oil until brown on all sides. Serve hot.

LEEK PATTIES & MEAT CUTLETS IN LEMON SAUCE

LEEK PATTIES

4–5 leeks
1–2 medium potatoes, peeled, or $\frac{3}{4}$ lb
  (375 g) ground beef
2 eggs, beaten
Salt and freshly ground black pepper
Flour for dredging
Oil for frying

Trim the leeks, and slice lengthwise, removing the tough inner core and green part of the vegetable. Rinse thoroughly under running water, bending the layers back one at a time. Cut the stalks into 2-in (5-cm) lengths and put these into a large pot with the potatoes. Cover with water, add salt, and cook until the vegetables soften, about 30 minutes. Drain. Transfer the vegetables to a large sieve and remove the potatoes. Allow the leeks to drain and cool. Squeeze thoroughly. Grind or chop finely (not in a food processor) and transfer to a large bowl.

Grate the potatoes or put them through a potato masher. Add the mashed potatoes (or meat if using) to the leeks and mix in the beaten eggs. Add salt and pepper to season. Mix until all the ingredients are well blended. Allow the mixture to rest for 1 hour. Shape the mixture into round patties, roll them in flour, and fry until golden on both sides. Serve warm or at room temperature with a squeeze of lemon juice, or a yogurt or dill sauce.

MEAT CUTLETS IN LEMON SAUCE

1 large bunch large-ribbed Swiss chard leaves
2 onions, chopped
Vegetable oil
1 lb (500 g) ground beef
2 eggs, beaten
$\frac{1}{2}$ cup (35 g) bread crumbs
Salt and freshly ground black pepper
Flour for dredging
Juice of 2 large lemons
1–2 cups (250–500 ml) clear bouillon (stock)

Rinse the Swiss chard and separate the broad white ribs from the green. Trim the bottoms of the ribs and place them on the bottom and sides of a large pot. Set aside. In a separate covered pot, steam the green leaves until they are soft. Remove. When they are cool enough to handle, squeeze firmly to remove as much water as possible. Chop finely. Fry the onions in a little oil until they soften. Add the chopped chard leaves and continue cooking for another 2 to 3 minutes. Allow this mixture to cool a bit and then mix in the ground meat, eggs, and bread crumbs, adding salt and pepper to season. Shape the mixture into small round patties, roll them in flour, and brown them in a little more oil on both sides. Place the cooked cutlets in the large pot on top of the chard ribs. Add the bouillon (stock) and cook over a low heat for 30 minutes. Squeeze the lemon juice over the cutlets and serve with the remaining liquid and ribs of the chard.

Leek Patties (left) with lemon wedges, and Meat Cutlets in Lemon Sauce.

ALBONDIGAS

Spicy Meatballs on Puréed Roasted Eggplant

In Ladino, a fifteenth-century Spanish dialect spoken by Sephardic Jews, Albondigas are small round meatballs spiced with lots of black pepper. Here they are fried and baked together with mashed roasted eggplant purée.

For the meatballs:

> 1 lb (500 g) ground beef
> 1 onion, chopped fine
> 2 tablespoons bread crumbs
> 1 egg, beaten
> Salt and a good amount of freshly ground
>   black pepper
> Flour for dredging (optional)
> ⅓ cup (90 ml) corn oil

For the eggplant purée:

> 3 medium eggplants (aubergines)
> Sugar to taste (optional)
> 2–3 cloves garlic, crushed
> Salt
> Freshly ground black pepper
> Ground almonds (optional)

To prepare the **meatballs**, preheat the oven to 400°F (200°C, gas mark 6). Combine the meat, onion, bread crumbs, egg, salt, and lots of freshly ground pepper. Mix well and form into plum-sized balls. For a crisper finish, the meatballs can be rolled in flour before frying. Heat the oil in a shallow frying pan and fry the meatballs on all sides until well browned. Remove with a slotted spoon and set aside in a bowl. Reserve pan with drippings.

To prepare the **purée**, grill or roast the eggplants (aubergines) over an open flame or under the broiler (grill) until soft. When they are cool enough to handle, peel and chop. Add sugar if desired. In the remaining oil in the pan in which the meatballs were cooked, stir the mashed eggplant over medium heat. Scrape the bottom with a wooden spoon to keep it from sticking. Add the garlic, salt, and lots of freshly ground black pepper. Cook for another minute and remove from the heat.

To assemble, transfer the eggplant to a shallow ovenproof dish and lay the meatballs on top. Press them down into the eggplant mixture, and spread on top whatever juice remains in the bowl from the meatballs. Sprinkle on a few ground almonds if desired. Bake for approximately 30 minutes. Serve warm or at room temperature, with fresh bread.

GARLICKY, PEPPERY FISH (HRAYMI)

Pini Levy, Pini in the Courtyard

In Jewish tradition, the Friday evening Sabbath meal includes both a soup and fish course, in addition to the main meat or chicken. Ashkenazi Jews (of Eastern European origin) have made Gefilte Fish (page 92), a carp dish served with horse-radish sauce, their tradition. Hraymi is a very spicy fish dish that became traditional among the Sephardic Jews who came from North Africa and Libya. Europeans might exchange their Gefilte Fish for Hraymi, but the reverse would never happen. "Hraymi is the love that has no substitute," it is claimed, "and the pain that accompanies it is the pain of love".

> 2 lb (1 kg) fresh fish fillets, such as bass or halibut
> Fresh lemon juice
> Salt
> $\frac{1}{2}$ cup (125 ml) vegetable oil
> 4–6 cloves garlic, peeled and sliced
> 1 green chile, finely sliced, or 3 whole dried red chiles
> 2 teaspoons sweet paprika
> 4–5 tomatoes, thickly sliced
> 3 tablespoons chopped cilantro (coriander) or chopped celery stalk
> Garnish: lemon wedges

Squeeze some lemon juice over the fish and sprinkle with salt. Allow to stand for 10 minutes. Heat the oil in a large frying pan that can hold all the fish slices in one layer, over a medium to high flame. Add the garlic and sliced peppers. As the oil around the garlic begins to bubble, add the paprika and salt. Stir gently and cook for another minute.

Remove the spiced oil from the pan and reserve. Do not rinse the pan. Place the sliced tomatoes on the bottom of the pan and sprinkle half of the reserved spiced oil and half of the chopped cilantro (coriander) or celery over them. Add the fish and top with the remaining oil mixture and greens. Cover the pan and cook over medium heat for 10 minutes. Lower the heat, uncover, and cook for another 7 to 10 minutes. Shake the pan often to keep the fish covered with the sauce. Serve with lemon wedges.

GEFILTE FISH

Fish Cakes Simmered in Vegetable Broth

In the past, women purchased live carp for the Friday night meal on Wednesday or Thursday and kept them alive in the bathtub. I can still remember my mother as she caught the fish, put it on the marble countertop, and dealt it a sharp blow to the head. I stood next to her, eyes tightly closed. By the time I opened them, my mother was already grinding up the fish. Traditionally, instead of cooking the fish heads with the cakes to enrich the sauce, one stuffs the heads with some fish cake mix, cooking these together with the cakes.

For the fish cakes:
  2 carp, about 2 lb (1 kg) each
  ½ lb (250 g) fillet of grouper or gray mullet
  3 onions
  4 cloves garlic, peeled and sliced
  1 tablespoon vegetable oil
  2 slices stale challah
  2–3 eggs
  3 tablespoons sugar
  1 tablespoon salt
  1 tablespoon freshly ground black pepper

For the stock:
  3 onions
  3 carrots, peeled and sliced
  1 potato, peeled and sliced
  1 celery root, peeled and sliced
  ½ teaspoon salt plus 1 teaspoon pepper
  1 tablespoon sugar
  Juice of 1 lemon
  Chrain, or Spicy Horseradish Sauce (page 36)

To make the **fish cakes**, have the fishmonger remove the skin and bones from the fish. Reserve the heads and set aside. Peel and slice three of the onions and fry with the sliced garlic in the oil until soft. Cut off the crusts of the challah, soak in water, and squeeze out the liquid. Grind the fish together with the bread, eggs, and fried onion and garlic. Season with the sugar, salt, and black pepper.

To make the **stock**, peel and slice the remaining onions, and place them with the sliced carrots, potato, and celery root at the bottom of a deep, wide-bottomed pan. Add 3 to 4 cups (750 ml to 1 liter) water and the salt, sugar, and black pepper. Bring the contents of the pan to a boil, then reduce heat to simmer gently.

Meanwhile, to assemble, shape the ground fish mixture into flat, round fish cakes. Lay them gently, one at a time, in the simmering stock, along with the heads of the carp, and cook gently for 90 minutes. Add the juice of a lemon and turn off the heat. When the fish has cooled, transfer the fish cakes and the carrots from the stock to a bowl, cover, and refrigerate. Pour the remaining sauce through a sieve into another bowl and refrigerate.

Serve cold, placing a fish cake, a slice of carrot, and about a tablespoon of sauce on individual small plates. Accompany with Chrain, or Spicy Horseradish Sauce (see recipe, page 36).

STUFFED SARDINES

Margaret Tayar, Jaffa

Margaret Tayar's stuffed sardines have taken on mythological proportions in Israel. It is worth a trip to Jaffa just to sit down to a plate of them. I remember well a day in 1993, when I found Margaret sitting in front of her restaurant sometime after the passing away of her husband Victor, a sad and lonely woman. She invited me inside to dine.

I tasted her amazing stuffed sardines, and thus began a relationship that has never ceased. The fish tasted of tears and longing, and I somehow realized how deeply Margaret invests herself in her food. I often sit in her garden and listen to her deep loud laugh, which rolls like the waves, looking forward to the delicious meal she will soon serve me.

12 medium sardines, about 2 lb (1 kg)

For the stuffing:
> **8 oz (250 g) fresh gray mullet roe**
> **4–5 cloves garlic, crushed**
> **$\frac{1}{4}$ cup chopped cilantro (coriander) leaves**
> **$\frac{1}{4}$ teaspoon nutmeg, ground**
> **Salt and freshly ground black pepper to taste**
> **Pinch of hot chile powder**
> **Flour**
> **1 egg, beaten (optional)**
> **Oil for deep frying**

Remove the heads of the sardines, open the fish with a small sharp knife, remove the insides, and debone. Chop the roe and mix with the remaining **stuffing** ingredients. Spread the mixture on one flat open sardine and cover with another. Press together gently to seal and dip in the flour and, if desired, in the beaten egg, before deep frying. Serve with one of the following sauces:

Sauce #1:
> **Juice of 2 lemons**
> **6–7 stalks mint, chopped**
> **4 cloves garlic, crushed**
> **Salt and black pepper to taste**

Mix all ingredients and pour over the sardines immediately after frying.

Sauce #2:
> **2 tomatoes, crushed**
> **2 cloves garlic, crushed**
> **1 hot chile pepper, chopped**
> **Salt to taste**
> **$\frac{1}{2}$ cup (125 ml) olive oil**
> **$\frac{1}{2}$ cup whole mint leaves**

Mix all ingredients except the mint leaves. Pour the sauce over the sardines and garnish with the mint leaves.

SAUTEED RED MULLET WITH RASHED

Tamar Ly and Ezra Kedem, Arcadia, Jerusalem

Red mullet, or barbunia, is one of the most popular ocean fish in Israel. Rashed, or garden cress, is a very special local green with a delicate spicy flavor, and is found in the open markets of Israel. Israelis whose families emigrated from North Africa use rashed lavishly. It is rinsed and dried and then used as a garnish. Arugula (or rocket) leaves can be substituted for the rashed in this recipe.

For the vinaigrette:
- 2 tomatoes
- 3 cloves garlic, crushed
- 1 shallot, chopped
- Juice of 1 large lemon
- 3–4 fresh za'atar leaves or fresh thyme
- ¼ cup (60 ml) extra-virgin olive oil
- Salt and freshly ground white pepper to taste

For the bean salad:
- ½ cup (100 g) white beans, cooked
- Olive oil for frying
- 1 clove garlic, chopped
- Pinch of thyme

For the mullet:
- 1 lb (500 g) red mullet, cleaned and deboned
- ¼ cup (60 ml) olive oil
- Flour

Garnish:
- 1 bunch fresh rashed or arugula leaves, chopped

To prepare the **vinaigrette**, quarter the tomatoes and gently squeeze the seeds and juice into a small bowl. Add the garlic, shallot, lemon juice, and herbs. Whisk these together and slowly add ¼ cup (60 ml) olive oil. Chop one of the crushed tomatoes and add to the sauce, along with salt and pepper. Set aside.

To prepare the **bean salad**, fry the cooked white beans in a little olive oil together with the chopped garlic and the thyme.

To prepare the **mullet**, sprinkle some flour onto a plate. Heat the olive oil in a frying pan. Dip each mullet in flour on both sides and shake off the excess. Fry the fish quickly on both sides and drain on a paper towel.

To serve, place a few mullet on individual plates, depending on their size, with a spoonful of white beans next to them. Sprinkle the vinaigrette over the fish and arrange the fresh greens beside them. Serve immediately.

PICKLED HERRING IN VINEGAR

Along with Gefilte Fish, Eastern European Jews also brought herring to the Holy Land. Recent Russian immigrants have brought new versions, and today herring is considered a delicacy by all Israelis. A perfect meal can be made with plain matjes herring fillets together with some pickled herring, served with hot boiled potatoes, sour cream, dark rye bread with fresh butter, and a bottle of schnapps or icy cold vodka. Other accompaniments might include sliced radishes, thin green (spring) onions, hard-boiled eggs, and some fresh lemon juice to sprinkle on top. Note that you can also buy schmaltz herring for this recipe but it needs to be soaked in water for several days to remove the salt. Matjes fillets also require soaking—either in milk or water—but only for about an hour. Ask your fish monger about recommended soaking times for the particular fish you purchase.

Boil 1 cup (250 ml) water and add the sugar, vinegar, allspice, and bay leaves. Boil for about 5 minutes, remove from the heat, and allow to cool. Refrigerate if necessary to ensure that the liquid will be very cold when poured over the herring.

If using whole herrings, remove the heads and tails, split the fish open, and remove the entrails as well. Pull off the skin. Slice, with or without the bones (the bones can be removed if desired by inserting a sharp paring knife at one end and pulling the bone from the meat in one piece). The two fillets can then be pickled whole or in thick slices.

In a dish or jar wide enough to hold all the fish, arrange the herring in layers, alternating with the thin slices of onion. Pour over the pickling liquid, cover, and refrigerate. The fish should be ready in 24 hours and will keep nicely for up to 2 weeks.

³/₄ teaspoon sugar
1¹/₄ cup (300 ml) white or wine vinegar
1 teaspoon allspice kernels
4 bay leaves
3 whole matjes herrings or 6 prepared fillets
2 large onions, thinly sliced

SLICED OCEAN FISH IN MARINADE

Eyal Shani, Ocean, Jerusalem

Eyal Shani, one of Israel's most talented seafood chefs, prepared this carpaccio of sea bass long before sashimi and its Spanish cousin, *costiza*, arrived in the country. He made it with razor-thin slices of sea grouper, marinated in lemon juice, olive oil, and coarse sea salt. When he discovered hot Japanese wasabi sauce, Shani added that to the dish as well.

3/4 lb (375 g) meaty grouper or sea bass fillets
1 teaspoon coarse sea salt
Juice of 1 or 2 lemons
1/4 cup (60 ml) olive oil
1/2 teaspoon wasabi paste, or to taste
2 teaspoons sake wine (or water)
Fresh fennel sprigs (optional)

With a very sharp knife, slice the fish as thinly as possible. Arrange the slices next to one another in a fairly shallow dish and sprinkle the salt, lemon juice, and olive oil over them. Dilute a little wasabi with sake or water and pour that over the fish as well. Sprinkle fennel over the sliced fish before serving, if desired.

MUSSAKHAN

Roast Chicken with Onions and Sumach on Pita Bread

In Arabic, *mussakhan* simply means "browned during additional baking". This particular dish, developed in Nablus over the years, is a good example of the influence of various occupying powers on the local cuisine. The Crusaders who invaded the Holy Land in the eleventh and twelfth centuries were meat and fowl eaters, and they often ate meats on a flat bread that both served as a plate and absorbed the juices of the meat. They appreciated the local herbs and spices, and used them generously. This roast chicken dish is one delicacy that resulted from the Crusaders' encounter with local Muslims.

1 large or 2 small chickens (about 4 lb or 2 kg)
Juice of 1 lemon
³/₄ cup (180 ml) olive oil
2–4 cloves garlic, crushed (optional)
Salt and freshly ground black pepper to taste
Pinch of nutmeg, cinnamon, and bahar or turmeric (optional)
2 heaped tablespoons ground sumach (rhus)
3–4 onions, sliced into strips
2 tablespoons pine nuts
1 lb (500 g) pita dough (see recipe, page 64)

Rinse the chicken in cold water and wipe dry. If using two small chickens, halve them lengthwise with a sharp knife and cut each half into two pieces. If using a large chicken, cut it into 6 to 10 pieces.

In a bowl, mix the lemon juice, ¹/₄ cup (60 ml) of the olive oil, the crushed garlic, spices, and 1 heaped tablespoon of ground sumach. Immerse the chicken, coating all the pieces well, and leave to marinate for at least 2 hours in the refrigerator. Roast in a covered dish at 350°F (180°C, gas mark 4) for about an hour, or until the juices run clear, and the internal temperature of the meat reaches 180°F (82°C).

In a deep frying pan, sauté the onions in the remaining oil until golden. Add the pine nuts, mix, and remove from the heat.

Increase the oven heat to 425°F (220°C, gas mark 7). Cut the pita dough into fist-size pieces and flatten each piece into a round about ¹/₄ in (¹/₂ cm) thick. Place the rounds on a baking sheet and bake for 4 to 5 minutes. Remove, but leave the oven on.

Lay half the fried onions over the pitas. Place the chicken pieces on top, and then cover with the remaining onions. Sprinkle with sumac and return to the oven. Bake until the top browns and serve immediately.

ROAST PIGEON STUFFED WITH GOOSE LIVER

Israel Aharoni

1 red cabbage, sliced thinly
3 tablespoons butter
$^{1}/_{2}$ cup (125 ml) red wine
2 pigeons, each weighing $^{3}/_{4}$ lb (375 g) with
    their innards
Salt and freshly ground black pepper to taste
Garnish: Cooked chestnut pieces

Stuffing:

2 shallots, finely chopped
1 teaspoon fresh thyme leaves
Giblets of the pigeon, including the heart,
    liver, and other innards
2 slices goose liver, 2 oz (60 g) each
Salt and freshly ground black pepper to taste

Sauce:

6 tablespoons (90 g) butter
Bones of the pigeons, broken and cut into
    small pieces
2 shallots, finely chopped
1 small carrot, peeled and sliced thinly
1 clove garlic, crushed
1 stalk celery, sliced thinly
1 bay leaf
2 sprigs thyme
2 tablespoons cognac
2 cups (500 ml) dry red wine
Salt and freshly ground pepper

Sauté the cabbage with butter, red wine, salt and pepper and set aside. Debone each pigeon with a sharp knife, removing the innards but keeping the bird whole.

To prepare the **stuffing**, chop the shallots with the thyme leaves and pigeon innards. Add salt and pepper. Sprinkle goose liver with salt and pepper and fry for 30 seconds in a hot pan. Cool and set aside.

To prepare the **sauce**, sauté the shallots in half the butter. Add the carrot, celery, bay leaf, thyme, and bones. When all the ingredients are softened, throw in the cognac and allow to evaporate. Add the red wine, bring the mixture to the boil, and simmer gently until the liquid is reduced to $^{1}/_{2}$ cup (125 ml). Strain and whip the remaining butter into the sauce. Add a pinch of salt if necessary.

To assemble the birds, fill the cavities under the skin and breast with stuffing and the slice of liver, and seal with a toothpick or wooden skewer.

Heat the oven to 350°F (180°C, gas mark 4). Sauté the pigeon in butter on both sides until brown. Place it in the preheated oven for 7 to 8 minutes. Spread the sautéed cabbage on a serving dish, gently place the pigeons on top, and sprinkle the chestnut pieces around them. Pour over the sauce and serve.

GRILLED GOOSE LIVER WITH POTATOES

Haim Cohen and Irit Shenkar, Keren restaurant, Jaffa

In a certain sense this is a quintessential Israeli dish, encompassing as it does the whole historical gamut of food in this country. Tahina has been a component of the local cuisine since ancient times. Potatoes and onions roasted directly on charcoals represents a method of cooking introduced by the first modern Israeli settlers, a method still used whenever young people gather around a campfire. Goose liver has just recently emerged as a major Israeli product.

Leaves of 1 bunch parsley
1 teaspoon olive oil
1 small to medium onion, rinsed but not peeled
4 small to medium potatoes
4 slices goose liver, about $^3/_4$ lb (375 g)
Salt and freshly ground pepper to taste
4 tablespoons fresh tahina paste

Prepare the parsley concentrate by rinsing the leaves and scalding them in a pan of boiling water. Strain and chop in a food processor. Strain the liquid through a fine strainer or cheesecloth then stir in the olive oil.

Rinse the onion and potatoes and wipe dry. Wrap them in aluminum foil and tuck into a hot charcoal fire for 40 to 50 minutes until soft. Heat a heavy iron frying pan over a high heat and quickly scald the goose liver in it on both sides. Sprinkle with salt and freshly ground pepper.

To serve, remove the aluminum foil from the potatoes and slice them. Put three slices of potato on each plate and pour over the fat remaining in the pan in which the goose liver was fried. Season with salt and pepper, and place the goose liver on top. Pour over 1 tablespoon of tahina paste. Unwrap the onion, and with a sharp knife, cut into four wedges (retaining the skin). Place one wedge on each plate next to the goose liver. Add a heaped teaspoon of parsley concentrate to the plate and serve immediately.

GOOSE LIVER CONFIT

Saul Evron, Yoezer, Jaffa

Yoezer is the name of a wine bar owned by food maven Saul Evron, who has been eating and writing about wonderful food for many, many years. From the goose liver that is produced in Israel, Saul Evron prepares a confit that preserves the liver in much the same way that Hungarian Jews once famously did. The liver is preserved in its own fat, a truly kosher way of preparing it that protected it from overcooking. Avraham Matzliach, the chef at Yoezer from whom I got this recipe, suggests serving some coarse salt and pepper on the side.

1 whole goose liver, about 1–1½ lb (500 g–800 g)
Kosher rock salt and ground black pepper to taste
2–3 lb (1–1.5 kg) goose fat from the inside of the goose, clear and firm

Soak the liver in ice cold water for 2 hours. Separate the two lobes. With a sharp small knife, cut out the vein that runs through the liver and remove the bile sac and blood vessels. If the liver has bitter green spots, remove them as well.

Place the liver in a deep, dry dish and sprinkle with salt and white pepper on all sides. Cover with plastic wrap or a towel and refrigerate overnight. The next day, cut the goose fat into small pieces and dissolve over a low heat, not allowing the fat to bubble or change color. When the fat has melted, strain it carefully to remove any pieces that did not melt. Clean the pot and return the strained fat to it.

Heat the fat again to boiling point and add the two halves of the liver. Be sure the liver is entirely covered in fat. Heat, but do not boil, the fat and cook gently for 12 to 15 minutes, turning the two lobes after 6 to 7 minutes. Turn off the heat, remove the liver, and allow it to cool to room temperature. Reserve the fat in the pan.

After an hour, when the liver has cooled to the touch but the fat is still liquid, lay the two halves in a dish in which they fit together tightly. Pour over the fat, cover, and refrigerate.

Serve the liver cold, sliced thickly. Add a little firm fat on the side to spread on bread or toast.

MA'ALOUBEH

Meat, Potato and Rice Hotpot

Ma'aloubeh is a traditional Arab dish of chicken or meat, mixed with fried vegetables and then cooked in layers with rice. When the dish is finished and ready to serve, it is turned out from the pot in which it was cooked onto a serving plate, resembling a large brown cake of rice. The potatoes, added on top of the pot, end up on the bottom.

3 cups (720 g) rice
2 teaspoons salt
4 lb (2 kg) chicken, divided into 6 pieces, or
  lamb cut into cubes
$\frac{1}{2}$ cup (125 ml) vegetable oil
$\frac{1}{2}$ teaspoon crushed saffron, or herb mixture
  (see method)
3 potatoes, peeled and cut in thick slices
3 carrots, peeled and cut in half lengthwise
1–2 onions, peeled and cut in thick slices
1 cauliflower, divided into florets
1 teaspoon margarine or butter
Freshly ground black pepper to taste

Soak the rice in cold water for an hour, rinse, and drain. Stir in 1 teaspoon of salt. In a deep, heavy pot, heat $\frac{1}{4}$ cup (60 ml) of the oil and brown the chicken or lamb pieces. Add 6 cups (1.5 litres) boiling water and cook for 20 minutes. Toward the end of the cooking time, add the remaining 1 teaspoon of salt and the saffron or herb mixture, made up of a pinch of ground cloves, at least $\frac{1}{2}$ teaspoon of freshly ground black pepper, and $\frac{1}{4}$ teaspoon each of ground cardamom, cinnamon, allspice, and ground ginger. Remove the meat with a slotted spoon, retaining the cooking water.

In a separate pot, fry the vegetables separately in the remaining oil: first the potatoes, next the carrots, then the onion, and finally the cauliflower florets. Remove each vegetable with a slotted spoon onto a separate plate before frying the next.

Grease a heavy cooking pot with the margarine or butter. Arrange the potatoes at the bottom, the carrots on the sides, and the cauliflower and onion on top. Put the chicken over the vegetables and sprinkle with freshly ground black pepper. Spread the rice in an even layer and then pour over the water in which the meat cooked. Cover, and cook over high heat until the rice has entirely absorbed the water, about 5 to 10 minutes. Keeping the pot covered, reduce the heat to minimum and continue to cook for another 10 to 15 minutes. To serve, place a large flat dish or tray over the top of the pot and invert with a quick movement.

JERUSALEM CHAMIN

Slow-cooked Meat and Bean Casserole with Bread Patties and Rice

The Jewish religion allows no work on the Sabbath, which lasts from sundown on Friday until Saturday night. Consequently, for centuries, throughout the Jewish world, the traditional Sabbath luncheon dish has been an oven-simmered pot of beans and meat and other additions that could be placed in the baker's oven before sundown on Friday and brought home to eat after the Sabbath morning prayers. The dish differed from culture to culture and from country to country wherever Jews made their homes.

One portion Chamin Bread Patties and Rice
(see recipe, page 131)
About 3 lb (1.5 kg) lean rib or shin of beef
$\frac{1}{4}$ cup (60 ml) vegetable oil
3 medium onions, sliced
2 cups (400 g) small white beans, soaked
overnight
Salt and freshly ground pepper
4 beef bones, with marrow
1 whole onion, including the skin
Salt and freshly ground pepper
About 6 medium potatoes, peeled and halved

First, prepare the bread patties and the rice by following the recipe for Chamin Bread Patties and Rice on page 131.

Wipe the meat dry. It may be left in a single piece or cut into large cubes for more convenient serving. In a large, heavy pot with a lid, brown the meat on all sides in a little oil over a high heat. Remove the meat with a slotted spoon and set aside.

Reduce the heat; add a little more oil to the pot along with the sliced onion; and, scraping the pot, fry the onion until translucent. Add the soaked beans, 1 teaspoon of salt, and some black pepper. Stir well.

Add the bones and mix well with the beans and onions. Add the whole onion with its skin. Lay the meat on top and add salt and freshly ground black pepper. Put the bag of rice on top of this mixture and arrange the potatoes and bread patties around it. Add another good sprinkling of freshly ground pepper. Cover the entire dish with water, bring to a light boil, and simmer for 20 minutes. Taste, adding more salt if necessary. The rice will have absorbed much of the water; if the water level has gone below the potatoes, add enough boiling water to make it up to one-third of the height of the potato layer.

Heat the oven to 300°F (150°C, gas mark 2). Cover the pot and bake for 30 minutes. Lower the heat to 200°F (100°C, gas mark $\frac{1}{4}$). and leave overnight until early afternoon (one or two o'clock) the next day. If it needs to be kept longer before serving, reduce the heat. To serve, separate the various ingredients into different serving plates. Guests serve themselves from each.

ROAST LEG OF LAMB WITH ONIONS AND GARLIC

When I invite guests for a really special and important meal, my choice for the most heart-warming main course is always this roast lamb, made from either a shoulder or a leg. The meat is cooked together with potatoes, onions, and garlic and seasoned with rosemary. The quality of lamb in Israel is so high that even someone who has never cooked before can't possibly ruin a good succulent joint.

Make sure the butcher does not remove the bone, even if this makes the meat more difficult to carve. The lamb is much tastier and juicier when cooked with the bone, and the final quality of the roast will be considerably better.

> **1 leg or shoulder of lamb**
> **5–6 sprigs of rosemary**
> **Coarse salt and freshly ground black pepper**
> **Olive oil**
> **4 whole bulbs garlic, rinsed but not peeled**
> **6 small onions, rinsed but not peeled**
> **6–10 small new potatoes, rinsed but not peeled**

Place the meat in a roasting pan and rub on all sides with the rosemary sprigs, coarse salt, freshly ground black pepper, and 2 tablespoons of olive oil. Tuck the rosemary into all possible crevices.

Heat the oven to 425°F (220°C, gas mark 7). Slice off the root end of the unpeeled garlic bulbs and lay them around the roast, together with the onions and potatoes. Sprinkle over them a little coarse salt, some freshly ground black pepper, and a few drops of olive oil.

Place the lamb in the oven with the fatty side up. After about 30 minutes, carefully turn it over and lower the heat to 375°F (190°C, gas mark 5). Baste the lamb occasionally with the juices that accumulate at the bottom. For a medium-cooked roast, bake about 25 minutes for every 2 lb (1 kg) of meat, or to an internal temperature of 130–140°F (55–60°C), or 140–150°F (60–65°C) final temperature, after resting. For a well-done roast, add another 5 minutes for each 2 lb (1 kg), or bake to 145–155°F (63–68°C) internal temperature; and add still another few minutes if you like it really well done. I never consider serving lamb undercooked or rare.

After roasting, turn off the heat, cover the roast with aluminum foil, and allow it to rest about 20 minutes in the oven with the door open.

LAMB KEBABS

One finds three different sorts of kebabs in Israel: Romanian, Bulgarian, and Arab. The difference between the Romanian and Bulgarian versions is small. Romanians add baking soda and garlic to the mixture, making their kebabs spongy and bouncier than those of the Bulgarians, which are soft and delicate. Arab kebabs are prepared with lamb chopped by hand together with onions, parsley, and other herbs. Pine nuts are often added as well. Kebabs of all kinds must be juicy, which means fatty. The meat should contain at least 20 percent fat, which, fortunately, mostly disappears into the open fire over which it grills.

Lamb Kebabs served with Yogurt Sauce (see recipe, page 36).

In Christian Arab cities like Bethlehem and Nazareth, the owner-chef will prepare the kebab directly in front of the customer, chopping and mixing to taste. One Bethlehem version follows.

2 lb (1 kg) leg or shoulder of lamb, finely chopped with a large butcher's knife
2 medium onions, thinly sliced
2–3 tablespoons chopped parsley leaves
1 teaspoon salt and freshly ground black pepper
Pinch of allspice (optional)
3–4 tablespoons roasted pine nuts (optional)

Prepare a good charcoal grill. On a large wooden board, chop the meat, onions, and parsley together into a fine mince. Add the salt, pepper, allspice, and pine nuts and work everything together. Shape the meat into long, fingerlike patties and roll these around a long skewer. Cook the kebabs on the charcoal, turning occasionally until they are well browned on all sides. Serve immediately with Tahina Sauce (page 35), or Roasted Tomato Sauce (page 35) or Yogurt Sauce (page 36).

SOPRITO

Simmered Beef or Lamb with Potatoes

The soprito is a long, slow-cooking Sephardic dish of beef or lamb in water. The result is meat that is browned, soft, and almost falling apart. The accompanying potatoes are softly browned as well and infused with the tasty juices of the meat.

> **Corn oil for deep frying**
> **3 lb (1.5 kg) shank of beef, shoulder of lamb, or chicken, cut into large pieces**
> **4–5 potatoes**
> **Salt and freshly ground black pepper**
> **Bahar Mixture of Cutlets (see page 31)**

Heat 2 to 3 tablespoons of oil in a large heavy pot over a high heat and brown the meat on all sides. Add 1½ cups (375 ml) boiling water. Cover the pot and bring the water to a fresh boil. Lower the heat to the minimum so that the water barely simmers and cook for 2 hours, adding more boiling water if necessary.

Peel the potatoes and cut into 1-in (2.5-cm) cubes. Deep-fry them in another pan until they are golden. Season the meat with salt, pepper, and Bahar Mixture of Cutlets and add the fried potatoes. Continue to cook for another hour over low heat.

MUTABEK

Sweet Sheep Cheese Pastry

This traditional Arab confection takes a lot of time and trouble, but it is well worth it. About eight sheets of store-bought filo dough, brushed with melted butter between the layers, may be used instead of the dough recipe below.

For the dough:
    2³/₄ cups (500 g) flour
    ¹/₂ teaspoon salt
    ¹/₃ cup (90 ml) vegetable oil

For the filling:
    About ³/₄ lb (375 g) salted sheep cheese, or a mixture of chopped nuts, cinnamon, and a pinch of nutmeg

For the sugar syrup:
    1 cup (200 g) sugar
    ¹/₃ cup (90 ml) water
    1 teaspoon lemon juice
    2 to 3 drops orange blossom extract (optional)

Confectioners' (icing) sugar

To make the **dough**, combine all the dry ingredients and add 1¹/₂ cups (375 ml) water. Knead to a smooth consistency. Cover with a damp towel, and knead again after 30 minutes. Kneading each time around 10 minutes, continue the process of kneading and resting for a total of 5 hours. The elasticity of the dough will make it all worthwhile. The intervals can be shortened or lengthened, but always remember to cover the dough with a damp towel after each kneading. After 5 hours, divide the dough into 8 equal portions, form each into a ball, roll each ball in oil, and cover with plastic wrap. Refrigerate all the balls for 12 hours.

To make the **filling**, rinse the cheese under cold running water and soak in a bowl of cold water for 2 hours to eliminate some of its saltiness. Drain and dry, squeezing to remove any remaining liquid, and crumble into a bowl. To make the **sugar syrup**, mix the sugar and water in a pot and cook until the sugar dissolves. Add the lemon juice, bring to a boil, and cook for about 7 minutes. As it cools, add the extract. Stir and set aside.

To assemble, heat the oven to 450°F (230°C, gas mark 8). Place a ball of dough on a lightly greased surface and begin to spread the dough with your hands. Stretch it carefully on all sides, keeping it round, until it is very thin, almost translucent. Do not worry if the edges tear. Fold in the rounded sides to make a square. (If using filo sheets, brush 1 sheet with melted butter and proceed.) Sprinkle one-eighth of the crumbled cheese or nut mixture into the middle and fold the edges of the dough toward the middle to make a smaller square. Place on a baking sheet. Repeat with the remaining 7 balls of dough (or filo sheets), and bake until the dough turns golden. Pour 1 tablespoon of syrup over each, sprinkle with confectioners' (icing) sugar, and serve immediately.

LAVENDER PARFAIT IN PASSIONFRUIT SAUCE

Lavender has many uses in soaps, sachets, and colognes. It also lends itself to superstitions; for example, it is said that a sprig in a woman's pocket will protect her from a scheming husband. Lavender grows wild in the hilly areas of Israel, in the Judean desert around the Dead Sea, as well as on the coastal plains, and its flowers have become part of local desserts. This recipe is a parfait with a unique flavor, perhaps the taste of the desert.

For the parfait:
   ³/₄ cup (150 g) sugar
   ¹/₂ cup fresh dried lavender flowers
   6 egg yolks
   1 cup (250 ml) whipping cream

For the passionfruit sauce:
   1 lb (500 g) passionfruit
   2³/₄ cups (500 g) sugar

To make the parfait:
Cook the sugar and lavender flowers in ¹/₂ cup (125 ml) water in a small pan over a low heat until the mixture becomes a clear syrup, about 5 to 7 minutes. Strain and allow the syrup to cool for about 5 minutes.

Place the egg yolks in the top of a double boiler or a bain marie and add the syrup. Whisk the mixture over boiling water until the egg yolks lighten in color and increase in volume. Whisk the cream separately and fold into the egg yolk mixture. Pour into individual parfait cups, cover with plastic wrap, and freeze before serving.

To make the sauce:
Cut the passionfruit in half and use a teaspoon to scoop the flesh into a saucepan. Add ¹/₂ cup (125 ml) water and bring to a boil. Boil for 5 minutes and add the sugar. Lower the heat and simmer until the sugar is totally dissolved. Increase the heat and continue to cook until the sauce becomes transparent, about 15 to 20 minutes. Transfer to a clean, dry jar; cover; and store until ready to use.

JAMS AND JELLIES

According to local custom, the way to eat any of these jams is to serve them in little bowls on a silver or brass tray, with cold water in fine glasses on the side. Of course, there is no reason not to eat them on toast for breakfast.

GRAPE JAM

4 lb (2 kg) long white grapes
10 cups (2 kg) sugar
5–7 cardamom pods
Juice of 1$^1/_2$ lemons

Grape Jam (top), Etrog Jam (middle) and Fig-Thyme Jam (bottom; see recipe on page 131).

Separate the grapes from their stems, split open, and remove the seeds. Place the grapes in a deep bowl, pour over the sugar, and allow to stand for 6–8 hours. Transfer to a saucepan, bring to a boil then cook for 1 hour, or until the jam becomes a clear red (white grapes turn red during cooking). Add the cardamom seeds and lemon juice, and continue to cook until the bubbles turn transparent and shiny, about 10 to 15 minutes. Transfer to sterilized, dry jars and close hermetically. The jam will seem liquid at first, but it will jell as it cools. If the jam wrinkles when you pour it out and scrape it, it is ready.

ETROG JAM

Etrogs are citruslike plants with a large, thick-skinned lemony fruit. They are one of the four species traditionally used during the fall harvest festival of Succot (palm, myrtle, and willow are the other three). Many people make Etrog Jam once the festival is over.

4 lb (2 kg) etrogs
Juice of 1 large lemon
7$^1/_2$ cups (1.5 kg) sugar

Grate the etrog peel. Cut the fruit into wedges, remove its thick pithy core and seeds, and cut into small triangular or oblong strips. To make the etrog less acid, scald it in boiling water before soaking the pieces with the sugar. Put the ingredients into a large pan, cover with sugar and lemon juice, and allow to stand overnight.

The next day, place the pan over a medium heat until it boils, lower the heat, and cook until the sugar totally dissolves. Increase the heat again and continue to cook until both the fruit and the syrup are yellow and completely transparent. Transfer immediately to sterilized, dry jars; wait 10 minutes; then close hermetically.

MILK JELLY IN ROSE SYRUP (MALABI)

Leon Alkalai, Fisher Mino, Bat Yam

This favorite cold and wobbly Levantine dessert is sold from vending carts in small aluminum containers cooled over ice cubes. Traveling Malabi vendors can be found all over Israel—on the beaches, at soccer games, and in the main bus station in every town. It has become so popular that today it is sold in the supermarket in modern plastic packages; it is even served in luxurious restaurants, the jelly swimming in a rose-scented red syrup. There are three ways of preparing Malabi: with water, with milk, or with sweet cream. This version uses cream.

For the jelly:

3 cups (750 ml) whole milk
1 cup (250 ml) cream
²/₃ cup (100 g) cornstarch

For the syrup:

2 cups (400 g) sugar
1 cup (250 ml) water
¹/₂ teaspoon red food coloring
Juice of ¹/₂ lemon
2 drops rose water extract

2–3 tablespoons pistachio nuts, peanuts,
    or roasted salted almonds, coarsely chopped
Vegetable oil
Salt

Put the milk, sweet cream, and cornstarch into a pot and bring to the boil. Lower the heat and simmer, stirring continuously, until the mixture thickens. Pour into individual soufflé dishes or bowls. After it cools, place in the refrigerator for at least 4 hours, or until it jells and chills.

Put the water and sugar into a saucepan and heat until the sugar dissolves. When it boils, lower the heat and cook for another 20 minutes, stirring all the while. Toward the end of the cooking, add the food coloring. Allow to cool, add the lemon juice and rose water extract, and mix.

To serve, turn each jellied Malabi out on a plate and pour a generous serving of the red syrup over it. Sprinkle over the nuts and serve.

ADDITIONAL RECIPES

Musbacha
Cooked Chickpea Sauce

Musbacha is another version of cooked chickpeas. The name comes from the Arabic word *sabach*, "to swim." See the photograph on page 43.

1 lb (500 g) chickpeas, allowed to stand overnight
1 portion Tahina Sauce (see recipe, page 35)

Garnish:
Fresh lemon juice
1–3 cloves garlic, chopped
2 hot green peppers
$\frac{1}{2}$ cup parsley leaves, chopped
Olive oil

Cook the chickpeas as for Hummus (see recipe, page 42). Place the cooked chickpeas in a deep dish and pour the Tahina Sauce over it. Sprinkle lemon juice, chopped garlic, hot peppers, chopped parsley and olive oil over the top.

Knaidlach
Matzo Meal Dumplings

If the Knaidlach are cooked in Chicken Soup (page 56), they expand and absorb too much of the liquid. Therefore, it is preferable to cook them separately in water flavored with a bouillon (stock) cube or salt and add them to the soup after they have puffed up.

These Knaidlach are traditionally made for Passover, as they use matzo meal, which is unleavened. On Friday of Passover week, women in Jerusalem traditionally prepare a Chamin (see recipe, page 112), which is prepared with Knaidlach, potatoes, beef, and marrow bones. The following recipe is for 14 to 16 dumplings.

1 medium cooked potato, peeled
2 eggs, beaten
2 tablespoons vegetable oil
Salt and ground black pepper to taste
1 cup (100 g) matzo meal

Grate the potato into a large bowl. Mix in the beaten eggs, oil, and 1 cup of water. Add salt and pepper to taste. Pour in the matzo meal and stir until all the ingredients are blended into a smooth dough. Boil a large pot of water with a chicken bouillon cube or a teaspoon of salt. With wet hands, scoop out a bit of dough and form into balls about the size of a small plum. Drop into the boiling water, shaking the pot to keep them from sticking to the bottom. Boil gently for 30 minutes and add to the Chicken Soup.

Tabouleh
Cracked Wheat Salad

Cracked wheat dishes are the specialty of the Arabs and Druze of Galilee in Israel, and of the Lebanese and Syrians. It is rare for a meal in any village in northern Israel to begin without Tabouleh. The salad is traditionally served with lettuce leaves, which are used as a scoop. See the photo on page 85.

½ cup (115 g) bulgur (cracked wheat)
Juice of 2 large lemons
Salt to taste
2–3 bunches parsley leaves
2 bunches mint leaves
4–6 green (spring) onions
3–4 firm red tomatoes
¼ cup (60 ml) olive oil

Optional additions:

Ground almonds
Pomegranate kernels
Chopped lemon peel
Crushed garlic
Sumac
Freshly ground black pepper

In a large bowl, soak the wheat in cold water to cover for 10 minutes. Stir. Drain and squeeze the moisture out with your hands. Dry the bowl and return the mixture to it. Squeeze the lemon juice onto the cracked wheat and sprinkle on some salt. Mix again and set aside. With a sharp paring knife, chop the herbs and green onion. Dice the tomato into small cubes and add these ingredients to the cracked wheat. Add optional ingredients if desired. Mix and add the olive oil. Mix again and add more lemon juice and salt if necessary.

Chicken with Mustard and Honey

Honey to greet Rosh Hashanah (the Jewish New Year) with a taste of the sweetness of life is a deeply rooted tradition. Honey gives a brown glaze and special flavor to roast chicken, especially when it is counterbalanced with a tart spiciness. The following is one of the simplest, tastiest, and most unusual chicken recipes of the new Israeli kitchen. See the photograph on page 103.

6 chicken thighs or drumsticks
2 tablespoons honey
1–2 tablespoons fine mustard
1 tablespoon mustard seeds or deseeded
    mustard
3–4 cloves garlic, crushed
Juice of 1 freshly squeezed orange plus its
    grated peel, or the peel of 1 lemon and
    ½ cup (125 ml) orange juice
1 hot red pepper, finely chopped, or a good
    pinch of cayenne pepper
1 tablespoon vegetable oil
2–4 apples, sliced into wedges, or a handful of
    dried apricots (optional)

Rinse the chicken in cold water and wipe dry. Mix all of the remaining ingredients in a bowl. Add the chicken pieces, making sure that the chicken is entirely coated. Allow to stand for at least 1 hour, preferably 2, in the refrigerator.

Preheat the oven to 350°F (180°C, gas mark 4). Arrange the chicken pieces side by side in an oven-proof baking dish and pour the sauce over. Place in the preheated oven and bake for about 60 minutes, turning occasionally, until the juices run clear.

Borekas
Eggplant and Cheese Pies

Borekas were introduced by Sephardic Jews who emigrated from the Balkans during the seventeenth century. They were then adopted and improved upon by the Ashkenazi German and Eastern European Jews. Borekas are customarily eaten for Saturday morning breakfast. In traditional homes, they are added to the eggs that have been cooked with the Chamin (page 112), alongside Tahina Sauce (page 35), or with a chopped vegetable salad. There are various doughs for Borekas: this one is a homemade simple, flaky dough. See the photograph on page 69.

For the dough:
  3½ cups (440 g) flour
  14 tablespoons (220 g) unsalted margarine (butter)
  2 tablespoons white vinegar
  2 tablespoons vegetable oil
  ¾ cup (180 ml) yogurt or sour milk (*leben*)
  Pinch salt

For the filling:
  1 medium eggplant
  ½ lb (250 g) crumbled feta cheese
  1 egg, beaten
  Salt and freshly ground black pepper to taste

To coat:
  1 egg yolk, beaten
  Sesame or nigella seeds (optional)

To make the dough, preheat the oven to 350°F (180°C, gas mark 4). Place all the dough ingredients in a clean, dry bowl and knead until the dough is smooth and pliant. Do not overknead.

To make the filling, pierce the eggplants skin, then roast over an open flame or under the broiler (grill). When it is cool enough to handle, peel, chop, and mix with the cheese and beaten egg in another bowl. Add salt and pepper to taste.

To assemble, flour a work surface and flatten the dough on it to form a sheet about ⅛-in (½-cm) thick. Cut out 4-in (10-cm) circles using the rim of a wide glass (or an empty, clean mayonnaise jar) and place a small amount of filling in the center of each. Fold each circle in half and crimp the ends tightly so that the dough will not open during baking. Or stuff and shape the half-moons with the help of a turnover gadget. Line a baking sheet with parchment paper and lay the filled crescents on it side by side. Brush the pastries with egg yolk diluted with 1 tablespoon of water, sprinkle sesame or nigella seeds on top, and bake until golden, about 20 to 25 minutes.

Spicy Chopped Salad

This basic salad is served with Pastelicos. See the photograph on page 71.

  3 firm ripe tomatoes, diced
  2 young small cucumbers, diced
  1 hot chile pepper, diced
  2–3 cloves garlic, crushed
  Juice of 1 large lemon
  ⅓ cup chopped parsley leaves
  Salt to taste
  3 ice cubes

Place vegetables and chile in a large bowl. Add the garlic, parsley, salt, lemon juice, ice cubes, and a little iced water and mix well. Transfer to a smaller serving dish.

Chamin Bread Patties and Rice

This recipe is an integral part of Jerusalem Chamin (see recipe, page 112)—it cannot be eaten on its own.

> 1/3 cup (90 ml) oil
> 1 large onion, peeled and sliced thinly
> 3/4 lb (375 g) chopped lamb (optional)
> Salt and freshly ground pepper
> 3/4 loaf of stale challah or other white bread, sliced with crusts removed
> 1 egg, beaten
> Salt and freshly ground black pepper
> 1 cup chopped parsley and/or cilantro (coriander) leaves
> Flour for rolling the dumplings
> 3 tablespoons oil
> 2 cups (480 g) uncooked rice
> Salt and freshly ground pepper

Heat the oil in a large frying pan and sauté the onions until translucent. Add the chopped lamb if used and sauté for a few more minutes. Add salt and pepper to taste and transfer to a bowl, saving the fat in the pan for the rice. Use half the mixture for the bread patties and the remaining half for the rice.

To make the bread patties, soak the bread in water and squeeze it out completely. Add half the onion and lamb mixture, the beaten egg, salt and pepper to taste, and 2 tablespoons of the chopped greens, if used. Mix well, set aside for 15 minutes.

Spread some flour on a flat plate. Make small patties from the bread mixture, roll them in the flour, and fry them in 3 tablespoons of oil until they are browned on both sides. Remove with a slotted spoon to a plate.

To prepare the rice, have ready a large square of cloth, such as an old sheet or cheesecloth, about 16 inches square. Rinse the rice, put into a bowl, and add the remaining half of the onion and lamb mixture plus the leftover fat from the pan. Add the remaining parsley or cilantro (coriander), 1 level teaspoon of salt, and pepper to taste. Mix well. Place the rice mixture in the middle of the cloth and draw up the edges. Tie with a string, leaving about an inch of open space for the rice to expand. Continue to prepare Jerusalem Chamin (see recipe, page 112).

Fig–Thyme Jam

> 2 lb (1 kg) fresh figs
> 6–8 fresh thyme sprigs (alternately use anise seeds or flowers, bay leaves, fresh za'atar leaves, or 1 tablespoon of black peppecorns)
> 4³/₄ cups (875 g) sugar
> Juice of 1 lemon

Rinse the figs, cut into quarters, and place the pieces in a deep bowl with the thyme sprigs or other herbs. Spread the sugar over them, squeeze in the lemon juice, cover with plastic wrap, and allow to stand overnight.

Transfer the contents of the bowl to a saucepan and cook over low heat until the sugar dissolves. Increase the heat to medium and cook until the figs start to break apart, about 1 hour. Transfer to sterilized, dry jars and seal hermetically.

INDEX

Albigondas 88
Allspice 31
Almonds, Green 32
Arak 31
Avacado Salad with
  Labaneh and Mint 50
Babbaghanouj 40
Bahar of Ambah 38
Bahar Meat Spice
  Mixture 31
Basic Eggplant Salad 39
Beet and Turnip
  Soup with Beef
  Dumplings 60
Borekas 130
Breads and Baked
  Delicacies 64-74
Bulgur 31
Burghul 31
Capers 31
Challah 31
Chamin 112
Chicken Soup with
  Matzo Meal Dump-
  lings 56
Chicken with Mustard
  and Honey 129
Chickpea Soup
  with Squid and Parm-
  esan 62
Chopped Liver 52
Chrain 36
Cracked Wheat and
  Lamb Cakes 82
Cracked Wheat
  Salad 129
Cucumber Salad with
  Labaneh 50
Desserts 120-126

Eggplant and Cheese
  Pies 130
Eggplant Salads 40
Eggplant with Feta 40
Eggplant with Onion
  and Tomato 40
Eggplant with
  Peppers 40
Eggplant with Pickle 40
Etrog Jam 124
Falafel 44
Fatoush 48
Fennel 32
Fenugreek 32
Fig 32
Fig-thyme Jam 131
Fish 90-100
Fish Cakes Simmered
  in Vegetable Broth 90
Fresh Za'atar Salad 46
Fried Peppers and
  Tomatoes with
  Eggs 54
Fried Stuffed Kibbeh 84
Garlicky Peppery
  Fish 90
Gefilte Fish 92
Goldene Yoich 56
Goose Liver Confit 108
Grape Jam 124
Grilled Goose Liver
  with Poatoes 106
Ground Meat Cutlets in
  Lemon Sauce 86
Hearty Lentil Soup 58
Herb-stuffed Pastry
  Triangles 68
Horseradish 32
Hraymi 90

Hummus 42
Jachnun 74
Jams and Jellies 124
Jerusalem Chamin 112
Jerusalem Kugel 66
Ka'ak 64
Kebabs 116
Kibbeh Mahshiyeh 84
Kibbeh Naaya 82
Kibbeh Soup 60
Knaidlich 128
Kugel 66
Labaneh 37
Lachma Ba'ajeen 72
Lamb Kebabs 116
Lavender Parfait in Pas-
  sionfruit Sauce 122
Leek patties 86
Ma'aloubeh 110
Malabi 126
Malauch 74
Matzo Meal
  Dumplings 128
Meat and Poultry
  102-118
Meat-filled Baked
  Pastries 70
Meat-topped Pastry 72
Milk Jelly in Rose
  Syrup 126
Mint 33
Mixed Pickles 38
Musbacha 128
Mussakhan 102
Mutabek 120
Onion Salad 46
Paprika 33
Parsley Salad 46
Pastelicos 70

Patira 68
Pickled Cucumbers 37
Pickled Herring in
  Vinegar 98
Pickled Turnips 38
Pine Nuts 33
Pita and Pomegranate
  Salad 48
Pita 64
Pomegranate 33
Potato Salad 52
Red Zhoug 36
Roast Chicken with
  Onions and Sumach
  on Pita Bread 102
Roast Leg of Lamb with
  Onions and Garlic 114
Roast Pigeon stuffed
  with Goose Liver 104
Roasted Tomato
  Sauce 35
Sambusak 64
Sautéed Red Mullet
  with Rashed 96
Savoury Noodle and
  Egg Pastry 66
Shakshouka 54
Simmered Beef or
  Lamb with
  Potatoes 118
Sliced Ocean Fish in
  Marinade 100
Slow Cooked Meat and
  Bean Casserole with
  Bread Patties and
  Rice 112
Soprito 118
Soups 56-62
Spicy Chopped

Salad 130
Spicy Horseradish
  Sauce 36
Spicy Meatballs on
  Puréed Roasted Egg-
  plant 88
Stuffed Foods and
  Croquettes 76-88
Stuffed Arthichokes
  with Agristada
  Sauce 80
Stuffed Figs with
  Gooseliver 78
Stuffed Sardines 94
Stuffed Vine Leaves 76
Sumach 33
Sweet Sheep Cheese
  Pastry 120
Tabouleh 129
Tahina 33, 35
Yemenite Breads 74
Yogurt Sauce for
  Stuffed Vine
  Leaves 37
Yogurt Sauce 36
Za'atar 33
Zhoug 36